FROM THE ZOO TO THE WILD

YOUR GUIDE TO ENTREPRENEURIAL FREEDOM AND WEALTH

CHRIS LALOMIA

Advance Praise

"Chris Lalomia does an excellent job of blending his personal story with sage advice for first time business owners. *From the Zoo to the Wild* is also a shot in the arm for entrepreneurs who've been out there and looking to jumpstart 2021 with tips, methods, and the inspiration to take it up a notch."

—Dr. Ivan Misner, New York Times bestselling author and founder of BNI, the world's largest networking group

"When I started my company, I would have given almost anything to know what I did not know. Chris's book, *From the Zoo to the Wild*, tells future entrepreneurs what they need to know. This is a must-read for anyone thinking about taking the leap."

—Dale Cardwell, consumer investigator, six-time Emmy award-winning journalist, Atlanta TV and radio host, founder of TrustDALE®

"Chris Lalomia's book rings true to the things my dad taught me growing up, things like *"Do what you enjoy and the money will follow."* It's true. If you're doing what you like to do, you'll naturally want to get better at it and as your skills progress your paycheck will too. Plus, you'll be doing what you like to do. Read this while eating lunch at your cubicle in the zoo. It might just change your life..."

—Dave Baker, Host of *The Home Fix It Show*, Atlanta, Georgia.

"The thought of being an entrepreneur sounds exciting and challenging and it's both of those and much more. It's also not for everyone. Is it for you? If you are considering this leap of faith, this book is an excellent guide to help you sift through the pathways to becoming a successful entrepreneur and take that leap into the exciting, challenging and prosperous world of building your own business."

—Tom DiGregorio, president/owner, AquaGuard Foundation Solutions

"Every small-business owner looking for great advice and direction or corporate person looking to break out on their own should read this book."

—Scott Specker, owner of Five Star Painting, Alpharetta, Georgia

Dedication

I dedicate this book to my Mom and Dad, Berta and Sam Lalomia. I had the benefit of growing up with parents who gave me a springboard from which to reach great heights. More than that, they gave me the mindset to solve problems and the encouragement to believe in myself and to keep reaching higher.

I also dedicate this book to my wife Nicolle and children Sydney and Austin, who sacrificed as they took up this journey with me. It wasn't always easy, and while they didn't ever go without, they stuck with me. My hope is that they will appreciate what I have done for them as a husband and a father.

Acknowledgements

I have always believed that the leader I have become originated from my parents, took shape during my first real job, and found greater definition the first time I became the leader of a team. I am fortunate to have had many influencers over the course of my life who have helped me grow to find success as an entrepreneur and to share my story with you. Each have left an indelible mark on my life with their advice and encouragement:

Father Richard McLernan—High School physics teacher who taught me to expect more out of myself;

Camiel Thorrez—who first encouraged me early on to take my passion and make it my play at work;

Vic Riden—who counseled me to always be professional;

Jerry French—who held me feet to the fire to take the leap from the Zoo to the Wild;

Troy and Della Stafford—true entrepreneurs who infected me with their tireless optimism;

Ken Cornwall—for his unrelenting belief that success can come from hard work and values;

KJ Cornwall—for reminding me to keep being fun to be with and I'll be a good hang;

Tom DiGregorio—who encouraged me to strive for more, even in the face of success;

Sandra Jansky—for her belief in my leadership abilities;

Fran Dramis—for raising the level of my altitude each time we meet; and

Jeanne Wyatt – for allowing me to raise my level.

So many more people have helped me that I could write another book on acknowledgements alone. But let's get through this one first!

Table of Contents

Introduction

Events change things, sometimes forever. The home improvement boom that began in the U.S. about 15 years ago just exploded over the past year as a result of the COVID-19 pandemic, which forced lifestyle changes for tens of millions of people. Social changes that first drew me into the Home Services Business were already in motion with telecommuting, children living with their parents longer, a huge generation of Boomers moving into retirement, and parents moving back in with their children.

As a result of the pandemic, more people are working from home now than ever before, and most recent surveys show that 67 percent of companies expect "Work from Home" to be long-lasting if not permanent.1

In less than nine months, 76 percent of homeowners in the United States have completed at least one home improvement project, and 78 percent plan to undertake at least one home improvement project in the next 12 months.[2]

Homeowners will rely on outsourcing the work more than ever due to time pressures, the skills necessary, and the tools required to complete the work themselves. As a society, we have become accustomed to letting experts take care of things that we used to do ourselves (home cleaning, clothes washing, grocery shopping, meal delivery, car washing, and yes … home improvements). The trend toward outsourcing is increasing each day.

Necessity is what's driving this boom, so it's not just a fad. People are going to be spending more time living in their homes and more time working out of their homes than ever before. Homes will become a much greater component of a family's lifestyle experience and will be worth their investment. That last point is an important one and one of my *Three Secrets of the Customer*.

The statistics support my thinking. In recorded history, this is the highest level of home improvement spending ever seen in the United States.[3]

I recognized this trend 12 years ago when I left the Corporate Zoo to fend for myself and succeed in the Wild. I'm here to tell you my story, and if you're an entrepreneur at heart, sitting in an office dreaming of being something more, this book is both a gut check for you and a treasure chest of advice and guidance that will make your Leap from the Zoo to the Wild a successful one.

This is the best time to be an entrepreneur, and better yet, to be an entrepreneur in the Home Services Business. Favorable conditions exist and will continue to exist for home services for the foreseeable future. My message to you is—come on in, the water's perfect!

My intention for telling my story and sharing my advice, tools, and tips is to help budding entrepreneurs get their start in the Home Services Business, or in any small business for that matter. Additionally, I want to help new business owners upgrade their business mindset and give them some areas to focus on and perhaps help improve their operational excellence.

Are you the right person? You may be one of those people who dream of escape, but deep down inside, can't walk away from the corporate life—with its steady paychecks, cafeteria, and IT department. I'm not saying that working in a company doesn't allow you to find personal fulfillment. Nevertheless, you may be sitting in your office or cubicle thinking about running your own show—on your own terms—and wondering if you have what it takes to succeed on your own.

You may be that person who's looking for something more. You have an idea and the confidence to make it in the Wild. It took me a while to realize it, but when I reached that tipping point in my mind, I began to see the signs everywhere. The fog cleared from my vision and it was a bright world. As soon as I reached that moment in my mind, I knew I was done with Zoo life forever. It felt that way for me then; maybe it feels that way for you now.

My purpose in writing this book is to share my story and inspire you to follow your dreams. But you're getting more than just my story. These chapters also share the path I took, the discoveries I made, and the tools I used to become a successful entrepreneur in the Home Services Business.

Here are the seven ways this book will be a treasure of GOLD nuggets for you by giving you the mindset and confidence to make the Leap, the plans and processes you'll need for momentum, and the habits you'll need to succeed:

1.   Define your purpose for wanting to escape the Zoo. If you're running away from something and not running toward something, you're destined to fail.

2.   Determine if you have what it takes Physically and Mentally (and by physically, I don't mean passing a cardiac stress test.). You'll find why these are the two most important elements in your self-assessment and what you'll need from each to make it in the Wild.

3.   Create a business plan that can serve many purposes, including helping you begin to ask the important questions of the right people at the right times, especially before you make the Leap. This includes the best use of mentors and why you should never call them "mentors."

4.   Realize that in Home Services, *The Customer Experience* is more important than the quality of the finished product itself. That's right! I also share <u>The Three Secrets of the Customer,</u> that once I unearthed, significantly increased my momentum and improved my net profit. Most importantly, these three secrets gave my technicians the confidence and competence to engage with the customer and be the true artists that they are.

5.   Aim for Operational Excellence by building good habits as you start to scale and come to terms with yourself on what your role will be. How not to be lulled into complacency, but instead be on the hunt for continuous improvement in your processes.

6.   Achieve and maintain Operational Excellence by documenting your processes and procedures, knowing your key performance indicators, and sharing your near- and long-term vision with your people. Give them something to digest and wrap their commitment around.

7.   Finally, discover how to find, manage, and develop your Wolf Pack of technicians—the craftsman who will ultimately get the work done. I've worked with many lone wolves over the years and have learned *Seven Lessons* in managing, developing, and coalescing these fiercely independent, freelance mindsets into a team focused on *The Customer Experience.*

Looking back to 12 years ago, when I first made the Leap from the Zoo to the Wild, I discovered that I had what it takes. The physical was challenging and difficult to navigate, but I always had the mental, and still have that self-belief, stamina, and self-affirmed positive attitude to punch through. Your positive attitude will determine your altitude—how much you can achieve.

I hope that you will find within my book the mindset, the plan, and the style of leadership you'll need to succeed. With the right attitude, you'll be able to reach the heights that you're capable of reaching. You'll be able to approach everything as just the next challenge and an opportunity to grow and succeed even stronger.

I also welcome your comments. If you think you've learned a lesson in your journey that I missed and you would like to share, I would love to hear from you. If you think you've made a bigger mistake in your business than I have, (I bet you haven't ☺) I would love to hear from you as well. Please email me at chris@thetrustedtoolbox.com and share your story, and if I can be of help in any way, I will respond!

1

Are You a Gorilla in a Zoo?

You miss 100 percent of the shots you don't take.

—Wayne Gretzky

It's funny where people have their epiphanies—their greatest insights. I guess it could happen anywhere and at any time. Mine happened at the Atlanta Zoo, pushing a stroller through the gorilla habitat. The compound really was impressive. A lush, green environment was made to look as much as possible like the lowlands of Africa, where Willie B.—the main attraction at the zoo—was born and then brought to Atlanta, Georgia as a baby.

As I wheeled the stroller around toward the back of the habitat, my family and I came upon a large plexiglass window, and when I looked inside, I saw Willie B., sitting there on a tiled box in a tiled room with blue walls and a red floor, eating bananas. There he lived, alone, with nothing to keep him company but a tire swing and a small television set. Three concrete walls held him in, with only one side open to the nature habitat.

I looked at him and thought, *You're the King of the Jungle?*

Willie B. in Atlanta's Grant Park Zoo.

Then it dawned on me, THAT WAS ME! I was Willie B., but in a corporate zoo! That was my epiphany that day, watching the Great Ape perform. It was a huge turning point in my life. Up until that moment, I didn't know what I didn't know. I always wanted to be the Entrepreneurial "King of the Jungle," but I had gotten sidetracked and intoxicated by performing in my own walled-in complex. Each day, I would enter the same confined space of my office and work on the same monotonous tasks, much like Willie B. in his cage.

I was led to believe that I was king of the jungle with my title and a well-furnished habitat. Trainers would even tell me, *"You're the King, Chris! You're doing great!"*

… with little knowledge or interest in what I was actually doing.

And people would watch me perform at my desk or at the white board saying, "Isn't he cute? Let's get him to make a face!"

Yet, me and Willie B. weren't kings at all. Our lives were defined for us. We were told what to do, when to do it, and how to do it.

That evening, all of those feelings welled up in me and I imagined what I could be doing instead of what I was doing. I scolded myself …

> *I could be more than this … I am MORE*
> *than I have become.*

I needed to experience what it was like to be outside the protection of my corporate walls. The stress I was feeling originated from others' repetitive deadlines being imposed on me and my letting myself down for not being more than what I became. It was staring at me on my weekly calendar. I counted up the schedule of activities and meetings for the upcoming week. It showed 40 HOURS of MEETINGS alone. And I was so trained, I had coded each meeting:

CYA—Cover My Ass or my group's ass

Status—Giving a status report or getting one

Justification—Justifying why someone should help me or why I should help them

As I looked over the upcoming week's activities, an unhappiness washed over me. I thought to myself, was this ME making a difference in the world? Was this ME competing at the highest levels? Was this all that I had become? I wanted more than this. I needed to see what I could do for myself, by myself. It was time for me to go … to break out.

At that moment, I knew I was done with zoo life forever. It felt that way for me then. Maybe it feels that way for you now?

In the same way city zoos protect gorillas from the uncertainties of the wild, corporate zoos offer people protection as well—but it comes at a price. If you're one of those individuals, you're letting your zoo-keepers define the space in which you'll perform and the parameters by which you'll operate. Whether you know it or not, you're allow-ing them to place a lid on what you can do and who you can be. It's understandable; they're looking out for their best interests.

The thing is, gorillas have no choice about their captivity. They can't leave. They're locked in. You, on the other hand, can jump out at any time! Or can you?

Maybe you're one of those people who prefer the zoo to the wild? There's a door to your habitat that gives you all the freedom you need. Maybe you have enough room to run and swing on things. Maybe you sometimes get to do what you want to do and it makes you feel as if you're in control of your life—that you're king for the day.

I'm not trying to say that working in a company doesn't allow you to do what you need in order to find personal fulfillment. When you work for a company, you don't always have to take your work home with you and the big decisions are left to others. You get to focus on being a member of a team and specializing in a skill of your choos-ing. You're given a great support network and you're rewarded with consistent pay and the ability to progress in a career. Your healthcare is well-covered and you get paid personal vacation time each year.

For some people, being pampered in the zoo is their definition of success.

I recently asked a group of successful business owners, all who had left the corporate zoo years ago, what was the one thing they missed most (other than a steady paycheck … ☺). The most common response was that they only had to concentrate on one or two tasks at a time. They didn't have to watch over and worry about EVERY-THING.

In a corporate zoo, you don't need to worry about everything—from making payroll to filling printer ink cartridges to making sure there's toilet paper in the bathroom. Your keepers do all of that, and they give you a paycheck, a parking spot, healthcare, a 401K, and some certainty that your job will be there when you return the next day.

At the end of my conversation with each entrepreneur, not one of them said they would go back to the zoo. They were all living the dream of independent business ownership: worrying about customers, hiring and firing employees, making payroll, and at the end of each week, hoping there was enough left over to feed themselves and their families.

If I haven't scared you off yet and you're still thinking about that sad picture of Willie B., then let's press on and do a deeper dive with some introspection I went through. It was time to GET REAL WITH MYSELF on what I wanted and what I was good at doing.

Struggling with My Definition of Success

I've never heard anyone say, *"I want to get to my cubicle first thing in the morning and work at my screen all day, produce reports, never see the results, go home, and come back the next day and do it all over again!"*

Yet, many consider that an achievement in their work life. Whether or not you're successful depends, I guess, on how you define success and on the trade-offs you're willing to not just accept, but embrace as you pursue your definition.

Some define success through their educational achievements, or by having a family, or owning their own business. Others measure success by the things or experiences they have acquired over the course of their careers, such as titles, corner offices, cars, homes, boats, or travel.

And for some, MONEY is the only metric.

Back when I was seventeen, the definition of success for me was to someday run my own business. And I kept repeating my mantra: I *hope* to run my own business … I *hope* to run my own business. I even remember what I had written down at the time:

> *I will own my own manufacturing company with 50 employees,*
> *making parts for the auto industry by the time I am 35.*

I kept that paper with me for years and kept working toward my objective. I thought I was making some kind of headway over those years, but I really wasn't. I never lost my purpose, even though I was on a path that was not leading me to my goal. I couldn't stop thinking about Willie B. and what I had become and how I had gotten so far away from my aspirations.

Not long after my visit to the Atlanta Zoo, I had a business trip to Orlando and was able to bring my family. So, naturally, what does a young family do in Orlando … go visit Disneyworld.

I love Disney! I love what Walt Disney built and how he set the tone for the greatest entertainment company in the world. When you enter Disneyworld or watch a Disney movie, it makes you feel really good inside. As you walk down Mainstreet U.S.A. toward the Castle, a sense of bliss blankets you. And as you look around, you imagine that everything is magical. It was for me, for right there on Mainstreet is where I had my second epiphany as my father's words from years ago came back to me and sealed the deal.

> *"Hopes are wishes. If you want to achieve something, write it down and make it your goal. Wishes only get granted at Disney and in fairytales."*

The ice cream hit the pavement. I realized that life isn't Disney, that this is the real world and that I have to get busy. I remembered that I *had* written it down, but I had forgotten about it.

> *That moment instilled in me the commitment and the drive to leave the corporate zoo forever ...*

That was the 'knot in my stomach' moment. After 11 years in captivity, I realized that I just couldn't have success; I wouldn't let myself get there mentally. And every time I got closer to feeling I had it, I wanted more things, more recognition, more influence, and MORE MONEY. It was not a good look, and I was not fun to be around at home.

I felt like Captain Hector Barbossa in *Pirates of the Caribbean: The Curse of the Black Pearl,* who, doomed to always being alive but in an undead state, went to bite an apple, longing just to taste it, but not being able to. Captain Barbossa expressed a very unhappy life:

> *"For too long I've been parched of thirst and unable to quench it. Too long I've been starving to death and haven't died. I feel nothing. Not the wind on my face nor the spray of the sea."*

I realized that I had been sucked into other people's perceptions of success and was not going after my goal of running my own business. I wanted to be significant, and even though I had a great lifestyle and family, the work that I was doing was not satisfying. I had no passion for what I was doing. But I had an inkling for what my passion was.

My epiphanies didn't immediately have me waltzing into my boss's office and quitting with no plan, no next step, and no way to support my family. I needed to take the time to figure out where the GOLD was out there in the world for me to enthusiastically stake a claim and mine.

At this point, I knew I didn't want to do what I was doing for the rest of my career, yet, at the same time, I didn't know where to go next. I hadn't spent a lot of time in manufacturing to develop any real skills. I didn't want to be the CEO of my own bank. And I didn't want to run a consultancy company. So, I started working on ME and digging into my drive, my passion, my strengths, and my weaknesses.

What Was My Passion?
I started asking myself, "What do I enjoy doing the most?" I took some time to jot down the things that I naturally enjoyed and could get lost in without effort. What makes me the happiest and would make the day sail by?

Well, I love sports, but I didn't want that to become my job—that was a hobby, from watching sports to coaching others. As I got older, I realized that I wasn't actively engaging in sports as much. I enjoy good food, wine, and conversations with friends, but again, that was the fun time, my social time after work. So, I took another approach.

I love solving problems, and even better, I love it when a team of high-energy people helps me solve problems. I like to take something that's big, hairy, and complex and figure out the solution to it. I've loved solving things my whole life. I've always loved the challenge. And today, I enjoy bringing teams of people together to muster their collective expertise to address and resolve an issue.

I love seeing TEAMS SOLVE PROBLEMS.

I was so into solving and fixing things that I majored in engineering in college—probably one of the best fields to enter for a young person with that mindset. While my first job out of college was in manufacturing—and I was on my way to my goal—it wasn't until my first big job at Andersen Consulting (now Accenture) that I realized that my talents and skills were in taking large complex problems, breaking them into small solvable parts, and developing solutions that would work in the end. I was so into it that I would find myself at dinner parties after work talking with friends about the issues I had solved that day, or was in the middle of solving. My energy level and passion would just skyrocket.

I'm also passionate about seeing results. I always enjoy seeing a new house being built – every element of it, from the development of the land to the design and architecture of the home. I love seeing how the vision-design-construction came together and manifested itself into an incredible finished product. Every aspect of home building was exciting to me, right down to the smell of new wood. I didn't just watch the construction on TV either. I would visit new home building sites just to see what they were doing and go to home shows to the see the latest trends in design and construction.

The last passion of mine is leading people. That one didn't come to me right away. For many in the corporate zoo, it's easy to dismiss employees and teams and just stay in their office or cubical all day and ignore people. I wasn't that way. I was always excited to meet with the people who reported to me and get status updates. (Remember me mentioning earlier the necessity for status updating in the zoo?)

I went beyond the standard approach though. I changed the structure of my team's updates and increased the energy level by keeping those sessions to 30 minutes with a three-part structure: What do you have for me? What do you need from me? ... and finally, what do I want from you.

That GOLD nugget of leadership passion stayed with me from the zoo to the wild and helped me grow my business. It also helped me realize that aligning peoples' needs with your wants is a great way to solve problems, get results, and move further on the journey to success.

What Are My Strengths and Opportunities?

All too often, people say, *"Work on developing your weaknesses,"* when they should be saying,

> *"Capitalize on your strengths and abilities."*

By focusing on your strengths, you begin to move in the right direction and with greater determination and purpose. Your orientation will be positive and not negative. Your daily activities will be completed more effectively and with more enthusiasm. You will feel more fulfilled and successful.

One of my greatest strengths is my passion for delivering excellent customer service. It draws like-minded people to me and to my Home Services Business—the kind of people who want to be part of something that is purposeful and fulfilling. Anybody who has worked for me can tell you that I expect a focus on customer service and satisfaction. They'll also tell you that they're rewarded for their efforts and for positive outcomes with our customers.

But what draws people to you can repel them just as easily and quickly. YES, YOUR GREATEST STRENGTH CAN BECOME YOUR GREATEST WEAKNESS.

Let me give you an example:

My passion for delivering quality work in peoples' homes does draw people to work for me, but it can also repel people. Recently, an employee left a customer less than satisfied with the work he did in her home. My passion quickly morphed into anger and I regrettably unloaded on him. I went off like a BUSTED HOSE! It was not my proudest moment!

I could have delivered my point calmly and logically, but I didn't. My strength became my greatest weakness—although my technician truly needed to be made accountable for what he failed to do. Of course, I say that to justify my actions, but at the end of the day, a different approach may have been better. LESSON LEARNED! He eventually lost his drive for customer service and left my company.

My passion to please customers can often become a weakness as well. When a customer complained recently about the home service she had received, I immediately went into Problem Solving Mode and did all the things I could do to fix the problem and make her happy.

At the end of the day, all my efforts to correct the work didn't change a thing. The customer was still unhappy with the job and wrote a negative review about my company (I'll cover positive and negative online reviews a little later in the book). My greatest strength turned into a huge weakness and it cost me a lot of money.

LESSON LEARNED! If you don't keep things in perspective, your greatest strength can become your greatest weakness.

Let's look at the other side of the coin now. What OPPORTUNITIES do I need to improve? Look, we all have deficiencies or shortcomings, or areas in which we feel the most vulnerable. But I've always viewed these as areas for improvement—as Opportunities. I've never viewed them as my weaknesses or others' weaknesses.

I was still in the zoo and had no idea where I was going, but I knew that I needed to identify where I needed to get better or be able to overcome my deviancies, because if I didn't, I would have wasted time and money.

I have two Opportunities that I constantly work on, with the first and foremost being FOCUS. I'm great out of the gate, like a tank releasing pressurized air. But I soon begin to lose steam and focus if I don't get the results I'm expecting in my short-attention-span timeframe.

My 'focus' opportunity led me to abandon one idea for a business venture in the wild once I realized that it wasn't going to work with the forecasted recession economy on the horizon. I was going to create a niche condominium product with some cool features and put it in the city of Atlanta.

The process would have included buying two houses next to each other and replacing them with a three-story condominium complex. It required understanding all of the zoning requirements, the construction components, and having a firm grasp on the projections. The mountain of required knowledge and development time was getting steeper and I soon realized that I didn't have the patience to wait this one out. Good thing too. I was hatching this condominium product idea in June of 2007, right before the recession started in early 2008. I would have been out of money and out of business before you could spell f-o-c-u-s. Boy, did I dodge a bullet on that one!

My second opportunity is my LOYALTY to people. This is a tough one for me to admit and actually write down, but has cost me the most money and caused the most stress over the years. I've even lost good people in my organization because I let the 'toxic' person stay around too long. I believe in people—sometimes to a fault—and have been guilty of giving individuals a third chance (yep, not just a second chance …).

It's a great quality in people to be loyal to others and forgiving of others. But when you break out into the wild to run your own business, it can mess you up if you don't practice tough love at the right times. When you're in the corporate zoo, your HR department can be a big help and make those tough decisions. They can help you see the toxic individual early and advise you on the proper process and protocol. But when you're out on your own, you sometimes just can't see the toxicity in an individual because of the momentum you're trying to build.

Probably the most difficult part of the process of identifying my strengths and opportunities was in finding the right words to define them. If you're like me and get stuck and can't put your finger on exactly what your top strengths and opportunities are, there are several online sites that offer aptitude tests to help you define them. One of the most detailed, thought-provoking tests I've found is the RichardStep Strengths and Weaknesses Aptitude Test.

Identifying my Strengths and Opportunities were the first two areas of self-examination. Next, I had to come to terms with what I liked doing—not necessarily the passions that I described earlier, but the tasks I enjoyed doing most … and more importantly, what I didn't like doing.

For instance, I know plenty of drywall guys. Their strength is in putting up drywall. They're brilliant at it. But most of them dislike working with the stuff. If you've ever worked with drywall, you could easily understand why. Pretty much nobody likes working with it, especially when putting up ceiling panels.

Here's another thing I'm good at, but hate doing: I'm good with numbers and during my initial self-examination, I even listed bookkeeping as one of my strengths. It took me almost two years to realize that I HATE BOOKKEEPING. I can't input expenses without losing my focus and trying to determine if the expense entry was correct or if there was a way of reducing or eliminating the expense altogether!

I used to go into the office on Saturdays when nobody could interrupt me to work on QuickBooks, and I can tell you straight up that nobody wanted to be around me for those four to five hours anyway. I was not a happy camper when making entries into our bookkeeping system.

Defining my Strengths and Opportunities and identifying and narrowing down my Likes and Dislikes helped me figure out the right business to be in, define my market, and nail down the best services that I could excel at and enjoy doing each and every day.

The next phase of figuring out what I was going to do required me to develop a framework for evaluating my ideas and allowing me to dream about what work life would be like out in the entrepreneurial wild. My decision framework would allow me to analyze the business ideas that I was thinking about getting into, and evaluate which ones to steer clear of, like the condominium product.

I formed a Strengths/Opportunities and Likes/Dislikes (SOLD) Decision Framework to provide a structure with which to evaluate my business ideas and potential directions. It helped me define the boundaries and the goals that would help me define success. My SOLD framework kept me from making bad decisions when I was seeking out the entrepreneurial path that I would take.

Once I identified my Strengths, Opportunities, Likes, and Dislikes, I placed them in my SOLD Decision Framework to bring me closer to understanding where my abilities and passions lie.

SOLD Decision Framework

<table>
<tr><td rowspan="2">Strength

Ability

Opportunity</td><td>Avoid or Develop

High Strength
High Dislike</td><td>The Sweet Spot

High Strength
High Likeability</td></tr>
<tr><td>Avoid Like the Plague

Low Opportunity
High Dislike</td><td>Areas Worth Developing

Low Opportunity
High Likeability</td></tr>
<tr><td></td><td>Dislike</td><td>Passion   Like</td></tr>
</table>

Your strengths are not going to bring you a sense of success and fulfillment if you don't enjoy what you're doing. Alternatively, you may have talents and skills that are underdeveloped but are areas that you deep down inside enjoy doing. For you, these may be areas worth developing. I've known entrepreneurs who've emerged from the *Areas Worth Developing* quadrant with successful businesses.

Finally, but most importantly, those areas that are your greatest strengths and give you the greatest personal satisfaction comprise your SWEET SPOT. Every living soul has a sweet spot, though few live and work in that quadrant. The ones that do are the most fulfilled because they found their PLAY AT WORK.

Find My Play at Work

Remember how you felt when you were a fun-loving, care-free, stress-free little kid, waking up in the morning during summer vacation? Remember how the summers then seemed to go on forever? You'd meet up with your friends and do something new and exciting each day. And the hours would just fly by, with you lost in play until the street lights came on and you had to go home. And after dinner, you'd dream about getting back with your friends the next day.

What if you could get back to loving to wake up each day and create something new? What if you could be doing what you love doing … for a living?

My first introduction to the concept of *finding your play at work* was while working at a machine shop before heading off to college. It was greasy, dirty, and hot, yet I couldn't have been happier! I was able to work with my hands and use my mind, and at the end of each day, I was left dead tired and sweaty. I was such a mess that when I would get home, my mother would make me undress on the back steps before coming into the house.

That was the first real job where I learned many valuable lessons. Yet, the most important lesson that stood the test of time and still rings true after all these years came from Camille Thorrez, the owner of the manufacturing company who would often say …

> *"Find your play at work, and you'll never*
> *work another day."*

I didn't appreciate or fully grasp the meaning of those words then. I was working hard and was probably feeling more tired from the work than feeling empowered with the "play." Looking back on Mr. Thorrez's quote, I did indeed work hard each day. Some days, I worked my ass off, but I loved it and I discovered that when I focused on what I did well, I did it very well. It came easy to me. You can be great at what you work at, but it's not "work" if you enjoy what you doing.

SO, did this chapter help you discover yourself a little? Are you a gorilla in the zoo, dying to get out? Do you have the entrepreneurial spirit, drive, and resilience to be that person who breaks free?

If you believe you are that person and the picture of Willie B. in his cage felt like looking in a mirror, you may truly be that person! If so, you need to TAKE A DEEPER DIVE INTO YOURSELF first before you decide to escape.

Get REAL with yourself, take the time to develop your SOLD framework, and start to dream about the big idea. Most importantly, make certain that you're running toward something and not running away from something.

Your first order of business: You've got to know where you want to go!

2
Leaving the Corporate Zoo

Get busy living, or get busy dying.
—Andy Dufresne, in "Shawshank Redemption"

After reading Chapter 1, you may have declared—as I did 12 years ago—that *"IT'S OVER!"*

You may have concluded that you HAVE to leave … that you don't want to be a captive gorilla any longer. But be careful, the negative feelings that are building up inside of you MUST NOT be what's driving you out.

Don't run away from the corporate zoo.

That's not what this book is about. I want you to run toward something. It's the positive feelings of joy in pursing your own thing that should be pulling you forward, even though you may not exactly know what that "something" is going to look like right now.

The zoo was all I ever knew and I thought I was on the path to success. Hell, I was already living the dream. Little did I realize at the time that I was running toward the wrong goal. Maybe it was the illusion that my gorilla habitat was the real thing and that I was the main attraction.

I was sitting at the head of the largest piece of granite in Atlanta, chiseled into a huge conference room table that had to be lifted by a tall crane into the fourth floor of the SunTrust (now Truist) building on Peachtree Street. They had to remove the big plate glass windows to get the monolith in there.

Talk about a show of power! I went from sitting at that table to sitting at the head of it – running meetings in one of the most opulent boardrooms in Atlanta, or in any city for that matter. The technology built into that room was state of the art. The chairs were the finest office furniture I had ever sat in. The trim work was incredible.

When I walked into that boardroom and sat down at that granite slab, I felt like the King of the Jungle. It fit me like a glove. I became intoxicated with the power and the gravitas of the boardroom and with my stature in it. But it didn't last.

From White Collar to Blue Collar
In short time, the facade began to crumble and I started to think about Willie B. again and with all seriousness, began to evaluate where I was and where I really wanted to go. I came to the cold, hard realization that my corporate career was no longer what I wanted to run toward.

Everything I had grown familiar with and dependent upon didn't seem real anymore. I felt like Neo in the film, *The Matrix*, with Morpheus trying to open his eyes to the truth,

> *"The Matrix is everywhere. It is all around us. It is the world*
> *that has been pulled over your eyes to blind you from the*
> *truth. A prison for your mind … I'm trying to free your mind,*
> *but I can only show you the door. You're the one that has to*
> *walk through it."* [4]

I never really wanted to be that guy sitting at such a grandiose table working for the zoo. I wanted to be the gorilla in the wild forging my own path. Moreover, I had been lulled to sleep in my pampered zoo life. This artificial world had its smart people, but it was also filled with people who weren't artists at all. (Although, some did approach "CYA" as an art.)

To be totally fair, I wasn't being an artist either. Far from it. Remember in Chapter 1 when I shared how I printed out my calendar for the week and realized that I had 40 hours of meetings? Not even work meetings, but 40 hours of either: (1) giving status, (2) getting status, or (3) covering my ass or covering my team's collective ass.

Those were the only three things I did basically, day in and day out! I wasn't creating anything. I wasn't attacking the market. I wasn't figuring out a better way to beat other companies and provide a better service to customers.

I had in me a passion and an affinity for creating great customer experiences, even though I had never run a business in the retail world. I BELIEVED though that I could be the best in the market and provide that service.

I reflected on my greatest strengths and what I liked to do most and started to evaluate ideas and options. I thought about starting a computer repair company or even starting my own bank (that was a popular idea in the early 2000s). I evaluated buying a gear manufacturing company which would have aligned with my goal back when I was 17: to own my own manufacturing company with 50 employees.

All of those ideas had shortcomings and eventually didn't work out, so I started working toward a Home Services company. That's the POSITIVE that I focused on—what I wanted TO RUN TOWARD. I knew that there was a better way to provide a great customer experience in home services and I wanted to be that person delivering it with a team of blue-collar artists who were as driven as I was.

That's what I was running toward. The big uncertainty was, COULD I BE THAT PERSON? Did I have the mental and physical stamina needed to be successful?

Maybe it is time for you to say you've had it. Maybe it is time for you to get to that outside place in the wild and experience REAL PERSONAL SUCCESS. But before you submit your letter of resignation and give your two-week notice, ask yourself …

Do You Have What It Takes?

I didn't know if I had what it took to make the Entrepreneurial Leap. I had been living at the zoo since I left college, and there I was in my thirties. I didn't know if I could just go out there in the wild and actually make my own way without a steady paycheck.

I was used to my keepers feeding me instead of me finding my own food. I didn't know if I had what it took to be successful. I had the power and the suits that a successful executive would wear, but I didn't know what it felt like to make payroll on a Friday.

I started talking with a number of small-business owners who were friends and willing to spend some time with me. I remember one conversation that really hit me. One business owner who had made the jump and started his own company 15 years ago said …

> *"You know you'll be successful when you can make payroll.*
> *Then you'll know you have what it takes."*

He continued … *"If you have a bad day in your corporate job, you still get to keep your job, collect a paycheck, and put food on the table. But not until you have to get in your car and drive to pick up a check from a customer and get it to the bank on Thursday to make the deposit and cover your payroll on Friday, will you know what pressure really means. Because people won't work for you for free."*

When I went to make the Jump, I had to be prepared to look after myself and my family. I had to make sure I had a good plan and that I could bring home the bacon, pay the bills, and take care of everyone.

There are two facets when it comes to knowing whether or not you have what it takes: THE MENTAL and THE PHYSICAL. MENTALLY, do you have the courage and self-confidence? Are you a risk taker? Can you solve problems? Do you have the ability to handle a number of things at once and the mental agility to pivot on a dime? Do you have optimism? Are you a good fighter? Are you resilient? If you get knocked down, do you keep getting back up?

I never thought of myself as a gambler, but after going through the self-analysis, I realized that all throughout, I always came back to betting on myself. If you don't BET ON YOURSELF and put your chips on the table, you'll never know.

That's the mental part and I think the most important of the two. You have to believe in yourself. I'm not talking about deceiving yourself – we'll cover that in Chapter 3, Your Escape Plan. I'm talking about mental resilience, stoked by a desire to succeed and the ability to work through both the good and bad times.

Next, PHYSICALLY do you have what it takes? I'm not talking about your health, although that's an important consideration. I mean, you've become accustomed to whatever your lifestyle is today and you may feel comfortable ...

But do you know how uncomfortable it will be once you leave the zoo?

I was uber comfortable when I made the Leap. I had a wife, two kids, and a steady paycheck. We had the big, beautiful house. We had nice cars. I had my eight suits. Yet, I knew that the family and I were going to go without all of the accoutrements we grew accustomed to for quite a while.

So, when I ask if you have what it takes physically, I mean have you saved up enough for the journey? We were in saving mode for almost a year before I jumped, and then I worked on my finances to figure out how long it was going to take before I could come back and come back stronger.

With all of my planning, I was still off by about eight months, primarily because I jumped at the start of the Great Recession in 2008. That's right. This King of the Jungle broke out of the zoo and ran deep into the wild at one of the worst times in recent financial history. I often joke with people by saying that when I eventually write my book, I'll recommend that everyone start their business at the beginning of a recession.

I'm just joking! But then again, my planning, packing, and preparing helped me work through the downturn in the economy. You've heard the saying, *"A rising tide lifts all boats."* Well, I was in a race to grow as fast as I could and get as strong as I could so that when the economy came rolling back in, I'd be on the crest of the incoming tide and everyone who owned a home in metro Atlanta would want to use my company.

You've heard those great stories of entrepreneurs going from bootstrapped funding to becoming millionaires overnight. Well, SUCCESS DOESN'T HAPPEN OVERNIGHT. It was 12 years in the making for me! When people I've known over the years look at where I am today, they say, *"Wow Chris, you've really made it. Way to go!"*

But let me tell you, those first couple of years really sucked.

What are you running toward and do you have what it takes? These are two important questions that I challenged myself and others with when asked. Once you have that worked out in your head, the next question is: do you have your spouse or partner's support?

Check in with the Family
If I were to go back to the idea phase before jumping, knowing what I know now, and doing this self-reflection piece all over again, I would have made sure that I talked to an entrepreneur (or as many as I could find) in the Home Service Business who were successful but also realistic— who've been through the start-up and the challenges of dealing with the general public in retail, and succeeded.

**IMPORTANT LESSON LEARNED: have SOMEONE
ELSE talk to your spouse or partner about your plan
for owning your own business.**

I would also have made sure that they talked with my wife as well before I jumped. They would have told her just how hard it was going to be. They would have told her how long it took them to be successful and the mental and physical sacrifices they and their families had to endure.

You can then come back with all honesty and convince them that you understand the risk, but that being a business owner in the Home Services Business is just something you completely believe that you have to do and can succeed at. You can let them know that you have the vision, the competence, and the confidence, and that you know what you're running toward.

If you approach your spouse or partner the same way I approached mine, you're going to try to sell them as much as you're selling yourself on your readiness to jump. But you have to make sure that they (AND YOU) are aware of what the physical downside will be, as well as what the upside could be, and that she/he has the same risk tolerance as you, because …

Nine out of ten startups fail.[5]

That's a hard truth to swallow. Why? Because very optimistic entrepreneurs need a dose of reality now and then. Cold statistics, such as nine out of ten startups fail, are not intended to discourage you, but to encourage you to work smarter and harder. To be the ONE!

Keep in mind that you're flush with optimism and your plans could sound like CRAZY TALK to someone else. Think about it: you're telling someone you're thinking seriously about walking away from a comfortable and accomplished job, a career with steady income, a healthy 401K, and lots of stuff.

If You're ½ In, You're All the Way Out

Let's say you want to do the "side hustle." You're thinking Home Services is for you and you're going to try it on the side, or you're going to run a house-cleaning company, or a maid service on weekends. You think you can get the best of both worlds: steady paycheck, 401K, health benefits, and the chance to roam free in the wild and make a little extra money.

Let me tell you, if you're halfway in and only partially committed, then you're not in at all. With "one foot on the platform and one foot on the train," you'll have the first leg of your journey filled with disappointment and disaster. A side hustle will never make the money you think it's going to make. Neither will it ever show you fully the opportunity to "be all you could be" with your great idea.

Now, with a side hustle, you'll always have that safeguard of getting a steady paycheck, so there's no real risk. You can make an extra five, ten, or twenty grand a year with a gig on the side. But gigs like that tend to peter out and fail because you're not putting your heart, mind, and soul into it. Actually, you'll end up splitting yourself in two, potentially compromising your position at work and never fully realizing the true freedom of starting and running your own business.

Now there may be some industries where a side gig could work, but SIDE HUSTLES DON'T WORK IN THE HOME SERVICES INDUSTRY.

When I thought about leaving the zoo, my definition of success in the wild was not just a couple thousand a month on the side. That wasn't it. My definition was to make a million dollars a year and build a strong, thriving business employing 20+ people. The journey you set for yourself may be different than my journey and my definition of success, but if you're seriously contemplating making the Jump, make sure you …

1. Check in with yourself

2. Know your goals

3. Confirm that the family is with you

4. Dive in all the way

If these first two chapters haven't scared you off completely, but have actually inspired you even more, then let's put your Escape Plan together and get busy living!

3

Your Escape Plan

A good plan, violently executed now, is better than a perfect plan next week.

—General George S. Patton

I must have inspired you. You're still with me!

You now know what you're running toward. You've set your goals. You have what it takes mentally and physically. Your partner is on board. And you're all the way in.

Chapter 3 is now all about your Escape Plan, your Business Plan. It's your plan for surviving and succeeding on the outside, and this is the best time to put one together—before your leave the zoo. As it did for me, it's going to help you create a focused mindset on what is it exactly that you're running toward.

If you're thinking of jumping with only a few ideas scrawled out on a couple of pages, then you're destined to be ONE of the NINE-OUT-OF-TEN who fail for not having flushed out all of the thoughts in your mind and all of the details. You're not doing justice to yourself or your family by not defining your product, your market, and your operations.

I'm not suggesting you write some long thesis, which reminds me of my high school English teacher who used to judge homework by its weight. She would sometimes say out loud …

"This one feels like an A paper.
It's got the weight of an A paper."

I'm not looking for you to write an "A" paper or go into endless writing and analyzing—what we often referred to in corporate America as "polishing a turd."

The value of your business plan isn't measured in its length, but in its reasoned ideas justified with numbers. Besides, the business plan itself isn't the end game or purpose of the exercise. It's the mental process you go through in putting one together. THAT'S WHERE THE GOLD IS.

So, learn to embrace the process as I did. My business plan gave real structure to my ideas and helped me begin asking the important questions of the right people at the right times.

These were the most important questions that helped define my business plan for the Home Services Business:

- What was the segment and size of the market that I was going to target, why them, and why me?
- How I was going to reach them?
- How I was going to convert leads into customers?
- How I was going to fulfill services?
- How I was going to run my operations?

Shop the Idea

The process of writing a business plan gives you the added advantage of being able to shop your idea and make it an even better plan. This is a huge benefit that shouldn't be overlooked. When you shop your idea, you're getting advice and feedback from people who've been there and often have more knowledge and experience than you do. I realize you may be concerned about asking for advice from "entrepreneurs." There's a good chance you're afraid to share too much information for one of two reasons, or both:

1. You believe they're going to steal your ideas.
2. They're going to challenge your thinking and either overwhelm you with new things to focus on, or completely deflate your balloon.

Regardless, you need to get your plan together and see how others in the space you're planning on entering react to it. THE GOLD is getting the feedback and ideas that they share with you that you can fold back into your business plan.

This process is going to help you fine tune and identify your strengths and challenges as well. I was able to identify where I could have a unique approach to this space and I could exploit that fact to my advantage. I was able to also figure out a pricing structure that would work. I also knew how hard it would be to convince people to use my service. When you share your plan with others, you get GOLD back and it doesn't cost you anything.

For example, if your plan is to open a plumbing company and make a million dollars annually in top-line revenue, you have to begin by knowing how much revenue one good plumber can generate in one week.

Asking the right people that kind of pointed question could help you determine the number of technicians you'll need to get to that top-line goal and how to best scale your processes and resources to meet the fulfillment demand. It's the process of filling in gaps, fine-tuning the numbers, and applying those nuggets of information that'll blast you out of the starting gate. That's why there's gold in shopping the idea and why your business plan is so important.

The exercise doesn't stop after you launch either. Your business plan isn't going to be written once and filed away. Make it a living document, especially in your first three years of business. I used it to track my progress and projections and confirm my numbers of handymen, customers, revenue, and net profit on a yearly basis.

Now that you've done the important groundwork, let's dive in and write your plan.

Bringing the Pieces Together

Many believe the purpose of the business plan is to secure funding by selling your ideas to others and convincing them to invest. There's no question that it serves that purpose.

The purpose of MY business plan was TO SELL ME FIRST. Remember, I was contemplating walking away from a career and a comfortable life. I had to make sense of all the pieces in my mind by having them come together on paper so I could comprehensively determine if my Home Services Business was going to work. This gorilla was about to give up being fed and being taken care of, so I had to know if I was really ready and capable of BETTING ON ME.

Speaking of bringing the pieces together, traditional business plans use some combination of the sections that follow. The Business Plan Template I'm suggesting here can be found on the U.S. Small Business Administration website. You don't have to stick to this exact outline. Use the sections that make the most sense for your business and your needs. In my plan for a Home Services Business, I used these sections. I'll share the value of each and how best to think about and complete each section.

Executive Summary

The executive summary may be the last section that you'll write, but it's the first thing you need to work through in your mind and get down on paper. You're going to be out there shopping your idea with people who are willing to give you a few minutes of their valuable time and share their experiences with you. You need to have your elevator pitch down so you can give them the short story with confidence and conviction.

If you're not ready to give an executive summary as soon as you sit down over a coffee, then you've already lost them. You're wasting their time. You're wasting your time as well for not getting the answers to the questions that you'll need to write your business plan. If you're not ready, you're going to miss the GOLD.

Company Description

I knew that my value, my business proposition, was to create a professional handyman company. Yet, I didn't want to just be known as Chris's Handyman Service. There were already so many small companies using the term "Handyman" in their company name and description.

If you have a cool name, then use it, but if it's not Gucci or Ferrari, then the company name probably doesn't need to be your own name. What it needs to be is a name that immediately translates your value proposition and makes it easy for people to remember your business. That's why I came up with **The Trusted Toolbox**.

I asked a group of ladies (my target market) to rank the company names that I had dreamed up, and honestly, what is now our company name came in second. Nevertheless, I did further shopping and concluded that there was GOLD in THE TRUSTED TOOLBOX name. I had to add the tagline "Home Repairs and Projects" to help define this new name, and the two worked out perfectly together in the end.

Your **Company Description** is the place to highlight your strengths. Go into detail about the consumer problems and needs your business will resolve. List the consumer segments your business will target. Explain your unique competitive advantages that will make your business stand above all other Home Services Businesses. Answer the most pertinent question: what are they doing wrong that you will do right?

Market Analysis

You're going to need a good understanding of your industry outlook and target market. Competitive research will show you what other businesses are doing and what their strengths are. I began by conducting global research on the market, but then quickly narrowed down my research to my niche (which can be bound by geography, service, or customer) and didn't waste time dreaming about the billion-dollar market. In your market research, look for trends and themes. What do successful competitors do? Why does it work for them? How are they operating? Can you do it better?

Now's the time to ask and answer these questions.

Your market analysis should focus on who your customer will be and what local market or markets you'll be serving. In my case, I knew it was going to be the Atlanta, Georgia market. And I profiled it down to four different avatars. An "avatar" is not a new concept. Corporations have been using "target consumer profiles" for years in new product development and positioning.

An avatar is a hypothetical profile that helps you figure out where your customers live, play, and work. It profiles such things as what your potential customers' hobbies and consumption tendencies are, which help define who your ideal customers are and where they reside.

I used the Claritas Research's Custom Target Audience and Segmenting Service.[6] I used their 52-segmentation breakdown and came up with <u>Four Avatars</u> for my business. I figured out the communities where my potential customers lived and worked, if and how they're involved with their schools and churches, what they like to do in their free time, and what drives their buying behaviors. I learned all of that and more.

What ended up becoming GOLD for me through that process was coming up with three possible names for my business and getting my avatar's answers to three pointed questions:

1. What was the name of the last handyman service that you used?

2. If you had to describe your perfect handyman, what would they look like?

3. What was the last project you did at your house?

I submitted those three questions, along with the three company names, to my Atlanta target avatar—an ALTA tennis-playing 35- to

50-year-old professional female. What a boon for me! The Atlanta Lawn Tennis Association is the top tennis league in metro Atlanta and that avatar happened to describe all of my wife's tennis partners!

Now mind you, tennis is not just another sport in Atlanta (… IT'S *THE* SPORT), and ALTA is not just another tennis league. It's currently the largest city tennis league in the world with over 80,000 members.[7]

I sent those three questions and three company names to my wife to share among her friends over drinks and appetizers at their favorite gathering place (of course I picked up the tab), and THE INFORMA-TION that came back was pure GOLD. I also learned how they went through the buying process for home services and what they expected when the technician arrived.

A big thing I learned was that NOT ONE OF THEM could remem-ber the name of the last handyman they used, but companies' names and phone numbers were in their phones for a quick call when some-thing was needed. That was why I selected the company name, **The Trusted Toolbox**, knowing that I would have to stay top of mind with my audience with a dependable message.

The most important thing my tennis-playing woman avatar (I named her Teri Tennis) told me was that she was looking for a great customer experience, and for her, that experience was more import-ant than the actual work that was being done. GOLD! If you don't deliver a great customer experience, then they don't care if the A/C came back on, or their hot water heater was fixed, or that the squeaky door stopped squeaking. The great artistic work your technician did doesn't matter if he …

1. Didn't show up when he was supposed to show up;

2. Didn't tell the customer what he was going to do and then just did it; or

3. That when he was done, he forgot to show the customer what he did!

I delve into *The Customer Experience* in greater detail in Chapter 4. It's so important in the Home Services Business that I devoted a WHOLE CHAPTER to it!

The GOLD HERE: buy some nice people who fit your target pro-file some drinks and appetizers and you'll get some great information about your market. Knowing this information will save you a LOT of money in misspent advertising dollars and will also help you center your operations on your key customers and prospects.

Organization and Management

The real value in looking at your organization and its management is the creation of a functional organizational chart. Here's the first one I put together for The Trusted Toolbox. As you can see, it had my name in every box except one—the first technician I hired. I was a one-man band with the vision of taking over the home services world—one $80/hour customer transaction at a time. I was President, Customer Service, CFO, CMO, Sales, CIO, and the first Technician.

The *(First)* Trusted Toolbox Organizational Chart

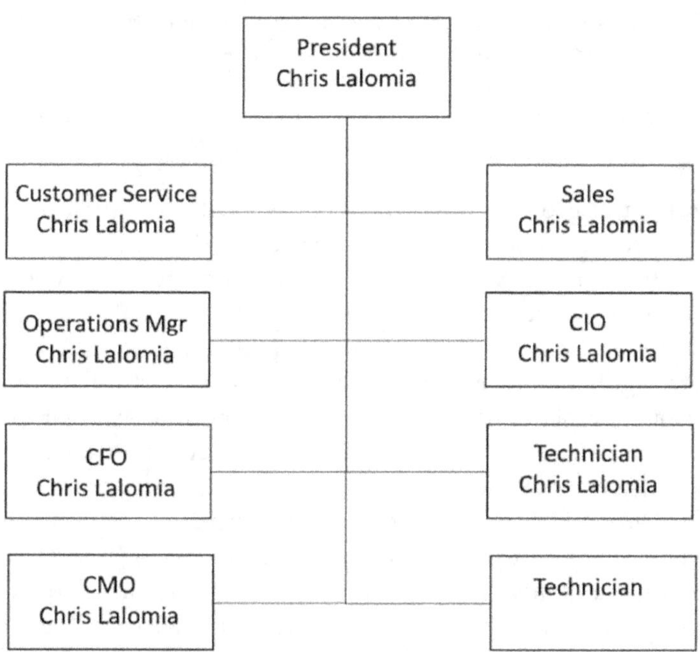

You need to determine when to begin to add to the team to scale your business. Begin with filling in the areas in which you're the least competent and/or you hate doing the most (think SOLD FRAMEWORK).

At some point, if all the pieces fit together in your business plan, you're going to need someone else to answer the phones, or run the technicians, or take care of the books. Believe me, those are the kinds of problems you want to have. If I didn't have that organizational chart above, I wouldn't be able to determine what role I was going to give up first, then next.

Service or Product Line

The GOLD here is in knowing where to mine. Niches bring riches.

In the beginning, my service and product lines were pretty much well-defined. When I went out to execute though, I found that I wasn't as disciplined in practice. I would do *ANYTHING* for ANYBODY at ANYTIME.

When you are out there in the jungle and you start running, stumbling, and bumbling, and without a well-defined niche to refer back to and ground you ... You will LOSE MONEY. I lost money wandering away from my niche! I would have done a lot better in my first two years if I had stuck to my company description and the line of service that I defined in my business plan, which was ...

> *I'm going to do small jobs that I know I can be successful at,*
> *so that I can <u>build my customer base</u>.*

I knew I could grow through the recession with that plan. And that when the economy started to come back and the tide started to roll in, I'd be that boat on the crest of that rolling tide because I had a customer base. With that attitude, I went from zero to 5,000 customers in three years, and today I have well over 15,000 customers.

Let me give you an example of wandering off. Early on, I was lured away from my plan with the opportunity for an apartment maintenance contract. The dollars looked awesome! But I knew enough to be wary of the "Shiny Object Syndrome" — glittery distractions that can affect entrepreneurs by drawing them off purpose.

If I had picked up that contract, I would have been buried in apartment maintenance and wouldn't have been able to build a customer base. Additionally, I wasn't ready scale-wise for that volume of work early on and at a smaller profit margin than I was planning on in my first three years.

It may have been steady income when I could have used it, but would have stunted or maybe even halted my growth, and I would have been scaling in the wrong direction. If I lost that apartment contract, I'd be screwed, without a customer base to absorb the blow. I'd be ONE of the NINE-OUT-OF-TEN. It was tough to turn it down, but in the long term, it was the absolute right decision.

Marketing and Sales

The GOLD in the marketing and sales section of your plan is in finding a way to get customers interested. How are you going to hook them and then convert them without blowing your whole budget on advertising, or worse yet, spend your nest egg? The work I put in this section helped me to avoid spending my seed money like a drunken sailor on leave and being left with no capital to operate.

Niches bring riches, and knowing your avatars and figuring out how to market to them will be key to your survival. To that end, you need to know the difference between these two approaches to advertising:

- **Relational advertising** builds your name recognition and puts you out in the market, but it might not make the phone ring or make the internet sing enough.

- **Transactional advertising** is designed to get the requests coming in, but identifying the right advertising vehicles that will reach your target avatar(s) when they're ready to buy your service is where the GOLD can be found.

Your brand and message need to stand out and help define your brand promise. Those are corporate zoo words meaning you GOTTA GET THOSE CUSTOMERS TO CONTACT YOU. You need to know your competition and how you're going to position yourself and stand out. Stay consistent with your brand and messaging and be ready to respond to a prospect request quickly.

There's a bit more GOLD in this area. You may believe you came up with the greatest name and logo. You may have spent thousands of hours and dollars designing and deciding on that perfect identity. But you know what? Nobody's going to remember your name, your phone number, or your website. You're going to have to keep hammering your avatar. A brand takes time to fill that vessel of familiarity in the consumer's mind and to become a household name. Spend some time on it, but don't become obsessed with it.

Once you have a prospect contact, you need to CONVERT that prospect to a customer, and that's all in your sales approach—and there are an untold number of approaches. The broadest categories are the HARD sales approach and the SOFT sales approach, which is more of an educated-consumer approach. Let's face it. We all want an educated consumer. They buy smart, but you have to figure out how to convert them into a sale.

Fulfilling on Your Service

We'll talk about Operational Excellence in later chapters, but when you're first beginning to operate in a retail environment and are putting processes in place, you need to answer these questions regarding customer fulfillment.

- How are you going to get the customer's information and then figure out what the need is?

- How are you going complete the service?

- How are you going to collect on it?

Fulfillment is the hardest thing to define, AND execute well, and FINALLY, SCALE. Remember, the goal is to get the revenue up to a point where you can arrive at the net profit you're expecting.

The GOLD mined here is in making sure you have enough processes to get started, then measuring performance to make sure you've got the right processes in place to fulfill your service. This will help you in PLANNING AND SCALING with the right number of employees and with well-timed investments in the resources you'll need to meet the demand.

My plan was to make a million dollars in revenue by my third year in business, and I calculated how I would get there starting with one handyman. I decided how I was going to price my services and determined how much revenue one technician could deliver in one week. Armed with that information, I was able to calculate how many technicians I would need and if my location, resources, and processes could handle the volume.

By the end of year one, I needed to have four to six technicians, and by the end of year three, I needed 15 technicians in order to reach that first million. Thinking through this before I started helped me to understand the lead, conversions to customers, sales, and finally, the costs with scaling up to 15 technicians.

Funding Request

In Chapter 2, I asked if you have what it takes from a mental and physical standpoint to make that jump into the wild. By physical, I didn't mean passing a cardiac stress test, but rather a financial stress test. If you're like most entrepreneurs, a first approach could be to seek outside funding from sources such as the SBA (Small Business Administration) or a venture capital group. For this approach, your business plan has to read very well.

Otherwise, you may have the resources to opt for the second approach—self-funding. In this instance, my advice is to go through the same rigor that you would as if you were seeking outside support. YOU'RE BETTING ON YOU, so your business plan has to be compelling and make sense to you first.

There were three sources of funding for The Trusted Toolbox. My first was the corporate bonus I received that year. The second was the savings fund my family and I had created. We set aside money for about 18 months before I made the actual leap. Third, I took out a line of credit on my house, which was risky, but I was betting on myself and the terms were only three percent. At the time, the cost of money was cheap, which worked in my favor.

The last potential line of funding was my retirement nest egg, and talk about puckering up with the thought of draining our retirement money! That was a REALLY HARD SELL to me and my wife. While I never had to do this, I can't tell you for sure if I WOULD have, but I probably would have gone through the SBA loan process before considering tapping more of my own funds.

I highly recommend not using the "family and friends" approach, unless you want them to be all up in your grill asking what's going on with OUR business. I wouldn't say NEVER go to family and friends, but if you do, be very careful.

It may seem a lot easier to ask your mom and dad or your best friend for a little money than it is to go to a bank and sit down in front of a lending officer, but it's not really. It's less personal to go the banker route, which ultimately will make your financial discipline stronger.

By going to family and friends, you're potentially buying yourself a silent partner (or two). Sometimes they're silent; many times, they're not. They'll believe they have the right to challenge your plans and that you should consider their suggestions. Imagine every family event turning into a business meeting.

Ask yourself: are you ready to have a partner when you sit at the table and BET ON YOURSELF? It might work for you, but in my Chapter 2 introspection, I said, HELL NO TO A PARTNER … I already had a wife!

Postscript to Funding Request

Let's say you've been successful in your funding request. Whatever the sources, the GOLD is knowing how to MANAGE STARTUP

FUNDING as economically as possible! Too much money and too long of a break-even runway doesn't make you efficient with your funding request or smarter in your spending plan. Instead, it may make you ONE of the NINE-OUT-OF-TEN who fail.

If you don't have the financial discipline to spend carefully, you'll run out of TIME, not money. What I mean is, you'll get to year two of your three-year plan and exhaust your timeline plan and everything related to it because you didn't use your money efficiently in the beginning. You'll never make it to your three-year breakeven point.

The GOLD here is don't get complacent over the amount of money you have sitting there in your startup account. Manage it as efficiently as you can, and then some, so you can get the outcomes that you're looking to achieve within a TIMEFRAME that you can live with.

Financial Projections

At this point, you have the BEST IDEA IN THE WORLD and a well-thought-out notion of what your topline revenue (VANITY LINE) is going to be by knowing those per-technician service revenues formulas. You're getting a handle on your real expenses and you're finding out what your bottom line (SANITY LINE) is truly going to be. This is like your engine room. Putting together your proforma or your financial projections will be key to success.

Don't be afraid to show your financial projections when you're shopping your idea. The VANITY LINE is always fun to talk about with people, but the SANITY LINE is where you want to get—with pointed questions to better understand present and future expenses.

A three-year projection is a good way to view these numbers. If you can show a break even within three years with what you're going to do and how you're going to scale up, you're destined to be the ONE out of TEN who succeed.

Once you break even and your net profits continue to rise, as in the graph below, scaling the business is going to cause your profits (SANITY LINE) to start to dip a little. You're going to be investing in resources, such as people, office space, and technology. Accept the fact that there will be an investment period for scaling up, and that realistically, that dotted profit line is going to look a little different than what you're expecting.

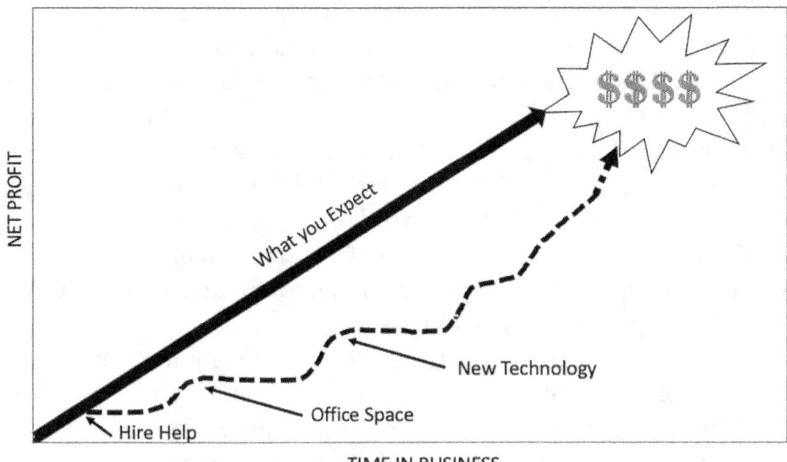

Double check your scaling-factor assumptions. Planning for additional expenses when scaling up will serve you well for when you go back to your plan to check progress. Have seasoned retail entrepreneurs in your business space review your numbers and give you specific feedback on investment costs and WHEN you should make those investments.

My approach was to always go for as long as I could until it HURT so much that I had to hire someone, get a bigger office, buy more vehicles, get better software … the list goes on. You will see in my list that it doesn't say, "Get a BIG GO-FAST BOAT for tooling around on the lake." My passion was in getting my business off the ground and not pissing away any profit on VANITY BUYS.

If you can make your investments for growth—as the above chart illustrates—and get back on your net profit projection line over the course of your three-year plan, then you know you've got something that's sustainable and you're ONE out of the TEN that will make it.

Shopping your business plan means you need to get someone to read it and give you specific feedback. I believe it's the very best way to get it refined and improved. Once you have it, ensure you have a steady flow of the wisdom and experience from other entrepreneurs as mentors.

Find a Mentor *(or five)*

Having a mentor when you're in corporate America means having someone help you successfully navigate the leadership of your team or the work that you're personally involved in. Many corporate mentors will even go as far as looking out for your career.

Mentoring in corporate America is a 'quid pro quo' kind of thing. You meet with your mentor with the hopes of furthering your agenda, but also with the intent of helping your mentor with their agenda. It makes sense; you both work for the same company. However, corporate mentors are different from mentors in the wild. They like living in the zoo and don't understand the wild or care to experience it. Talking with them is different than talking with entrepreneurs running their own businesses. You have to be careful not to threaten corporate mentors or challenge their pampered life.

For instance, you would never show a corporate mentor how you're going to make a million dollars working in the zoo. They would feel threatened and clam up and not share any information or show support. Some will even assume you're after their job.

JUNGLE MENTORS are different animals though. Their attitude is,

"This jungle is big enough for both of us. Best of luck!"

It is a jungle out there, and someone with experience, especially in the industry you're considering leaping into, will save you time and money with their knowledge and advice. You'll need help from people who have been there before. Having a mentor or two, or more, is probably more important than anything other than your business plan.

But it's all in your approach—that will determine whether or not you can land a great mentor.

Tim Ferriss is a well-known entrepreneur, investor, and author whose podcast series, The Tim Ferriss Show, rates as the #1 business podcast of all of Apple Podcasts. Ferriss "deconstructs" world-class performers across a number of areas, such as investing, sports, business, and art, to extract the tools and routines you can use in your business. He also offers great advice on how to approach someone to be your mentor.

GOLD: NEVER ASK A BUSINESS OWNER TO BE YOUR MENTOR

That's called free consulting, and no one wants to impart their wisdom and be your personal consultant … for FREE. Yet successful people will love to tell you about themselves and their realizations and victories if asked the right way. Offer to buy them a coffee, or lunch if they have the time, and show interest in their journey.

Everyone likes to have their egos stroked, but they are also willing to give of their time as long as you're interesting. By that I mean you're interesting if you're sharp-witted, personable, socially aware, conversational, and positive-minded. You're also interesting when you show interest in them!

Ask the kinds of questions that allow them to share how they saved a customer, hired a great employee, or broke into a new niche on a shoestring budget. They'll tell stories filled with GOLD nuggets of valuable information. If you ask the right questions, they might even tell you how the BEAR ate them and the mistakes or lessons they learned. Because as the saying goes, *"Sometimes you eat the bear; sometimes the bear eats you."* THAT'S WHERE THE GOLD IS.

DO YOUR PART. Using your business plan as a guide, prepare purposeful, well-thought-out, pointed questions so you can get detailed answers in return. Use their time wisely and don't abuse the help that you're seeking. The mentor's answers to your detailed questions will allow you to reinforce the strengths in your plan while also highlighting the gaps. A mentor's help in defining these for you and helping you through your issues and opportunities will help make you a stronger leader and a better business operator.

Make sure to ask if they'd be willing to read your business plan and if you can ask them questions on an as-needed basis. Staying in touch with mentors doesn't have to be continuous, but it's best if they can be at the ready for you if something arises or changes and you need their advice. So, don't become strangers.

What I learned from shopping my plan is that you don't have to have the best business idea. You just have to operate excellently on your idea. If you can do that, you'll be ONE of the TEN that makes it.

THAT'S A BIG IDEA and the thought to hold on to as you write your plan and plan your jump. You just have to be able to OPERATE BETTER than everybody else in your market.

So, where do you find mentors … (and remember not to call them that ☺)

The Networking Advantage
There is a lot of networking that takes place outside of corporate America, and if you've been a captive gorilla, you most likely aren't aware of all the activity that goes on in the wild.

Out in the wild, you'll find that people are flocking together all the time in their networking groups or "meet ups," which is a popular phrase. Your Chamber of Commerce is a great place to start. There, you'll find all kinds of organized events in your local area.

Find your Flock, they're out there.

It's going to feel odd initially. You're going to feel as if people are being forced to engage in conversation. It might even feel cult-like. And you're going to find that people are either good at networking or they're just trying to sell you their services and waste your time.

Networking is not just passing out business cards and pitching people, it is a skill that can be developed and it helped me get great insights during my first three years and still brings me great insights today.

One group that's helped me considerably is BNI (Business Network International), a global Closed Contact networking group. It's very structured and initially seemed a little forced and contrived, but it really started to maximize my time by helping me to discover what other business owners were doing and finding good groups to be a part of—which helps with the loneliness of going out in the wild.

I met business owners who were in the franchise world who shared valuable information about the franchise system and I used that knowledge to improve my own system. I started to find networking contacts that actually fed me business because we were doing complementary work and we could refer each other. I started to build up my expertise in networking, and it became a self-fulfilling prophecy of using networking to find other people who could not only help me grow my business, but could also help refer business to me.

Find one or two networking groups and do a lot with them. Attend the sessions and talk with other business owners and listen to their stories and share ideas for an hour and a half a week. It will allow you to disconnect from all the issues of the day running your business and you will get to talk with people who are like you, making their way in the wild.

My group meets for an hour and a half once a week, and I use the time to recharge my batteries. It feeds my entrepreneurial leadership and vision. I'll bet it'll do the same for you. Surround yourself with positive net worth go-getters.

You're rolling now! Your Escape Plan should be taking shape. You have your elevator pitch for shopping your idea to business owners. You know your value proposition and have a handle on your product and service lines. You're analyzing the market to determine your customer avatars. And you have a strategy in place for funding. Moreover, you've found valuable people who can give you suggestions and advice to help refine your plan.

If you've decided on the Home Services Retail Market and you're ready to jump, you're now ready to do some mining with me for what I believe to be the biggest GOLD nugget out there: *The Customer Experience*. In the Home Services Business, your customer's experience with you and your company is more important than the quality of the work itself.

4

The Customer Experience

*Quality in a service or product is
not what you put into it.
It is what the customer gets out of it.*

—Peter Drucker

"They're Cheap, Lazy, and Stupid!"

A Home Services Business owner told me that once and I never forgot it. Not exactly a banner slogan to wave around the marketplace. Not a winning attitude! If you or your people have that mindset, especially in the retail world, I can almost guarantee that you'll be ONE of the NINE-OUT-OF-TEN that fails and not the ONE that succeeds.

If you're going to jump in and work with the general public, especially in the arena of Home Services, the one thing that will make you stand out will be your understanding of the importance of *The Customer Experience* and delivering on it. BUT first, to address that mindset …

They're Not Cheap

They're just looking for value. They're trading their money for a service they'll value based on what it is worth to them, not based on the craftsmanship of whatever you're building, fixing, or remodeling. It's what they perceive the value to be, not what you think it is or a neighbor thinks it is. They are VALUE oriented … but that's not code for CHEAP.

One customer believed that having a dog door in her dining room for her incontinent dog was worth a thousand dollars. Now, many people hearing that might think, *"I'm not paying a thousand dollars for my dog to have a door put in a wall to go outside. I'll just let him out."*

But you don't know the experience she was hoping to achieve for herself and her dog with that door. She cherished that door because it meant her dog could go outside whenever he needed to without her having to get up every hour throughout the night to let him out. She

VALUED that project and was thrilled with the outcome. It helped her dog relieve himself and it relieved her of having to be on call 24/7.

They're Not Lazy

But they're for sure looking for good, EASY service. They have a lot going on in their lives, they're busy, time is stretched thin, and they need to get something fixed, changed, or improved, and they don't have the skill or the time to do it themselves. They want to hit that EASY BUTTON. They want to be able to make a call and have it done and forgotten.

My 47-year-old ALTA mom avatar in Alpharetta, Georgia is not lazy. Believe me. This is a very active avatar with more than tennis balls to juggle. Many have careers AND are involved in their children's lives AND belong to clubs. I can hear my avatar Teri Tennis now ...

> *"Everything else in my life is hard. Don't make this hard too because I'm already dreading the fact that you're coming to work in my house."*

For some people, having work done on their homes is a terrifying thought. They're letting somebody enter their personal space, and that's very off-putting for a lot of people. They're going to be inconvenienced and there's going to be dust everywhere. They're afraid something's going to go wrong or that the workers are going to leave a mess. You and your company need to be prepared for people who were looking for the EASY button, but are expecting a horrible experience.

They're Not Stupid

They are CHRONICALLY UNINFORMED though. Many will have unrealistic expectations. Many will think just because they watch HGTV, they can have a new tiled shower installed between commercials. Their expectations have been set to IMMEDIATE and EASY by the flood of information available. Some of the best lines I've heard start with,

> *"Well, I saw it on You Tube ..." or "I Googled it ..."*

Which in their minds translates to, *"It can't be that difficult to do and shouldn't cost that much."*

This reminds me of the time I had my very first website for The

Trusted Toolbox developed. I had no idea how long it would take or how much it would cost, but as with everything else, it took 2X longer than I expected and cost double what I thought it would. LESSON LEARNED.

When I started getting my first bids for the online site, I thought … *"Get out of here! That's crazy! I'll go do it myself."*

So, I tried to do it myself. But one look at WordPress Website Builder and I was DUN' DONE! The GOLD here is that you can't be the expert, and neither can your customer, but you want to EDUCATE your CONSUMER, because that makes the BEST CUSTOMER.

If you change your mindset from *"They're cheap, lazy, and stupid,"* to

"I need to help educate them to make a smart buying decision that will be the least stressful path for them in the long run," then the customer will choose you. They want to go with somebody who makes them feel good about what they're embarking on. And you have to give them a good, solid feeling that your technicians know what they're doing.

The Customer Experience

The Customer Experience is MORE important than the quality of the work itself. THIS IS TRUTH. The GOLD here: customers want to feel good about the entire process and will even overlook the quality finish of your product or service … if they FEEL GOOD.

I'm not saying you should finish with poor quality. That's a slippery slope. Your passion should always be to deliver a quality product or service. The customer's experience of your team being there and making a problem go away or making something better has to feel good or you will not build customer loyalty and attract more customers to your company.

It's been said that people will remember 97 percent of how they FELT when you were talking to them and will only remember three percent of WHAT you were saying. Translating this into Home Services delivery, customers will remember how they felt as you finished the work. And while you HOPE that the quality will be the lasting memory, it has to be the entire process to get you to the holy grail of repeat customers and Five-Star reviews.

I think the poet Maya Angelou put this best when she said, "I've learned that people will forget what you said, people will forget what you did, but people will never forget how you made them feel."

Some Bells You Just Can't Un-Ring

I remember my crew completing a small hall bathroom installation for a young Millennial that didn't go well. I had to fire one of my technicians and bring in another. Ultimately, I had to involve my highly-skilled operations manager to complete the job. We finally finished the job and it was up to me (the owner) to go and have the final meeting.

I did the final walkthrough and review and that bathroom was completed to perfection. It took an extra week, but I was happy with the outcome. When I asked the young person to let me know what she thought on the finished bathroom, she sighed and said,

"Yes, it looks fine, but I will not be able to share this on Instagram or Pinterest because this entire experience has been horrible and has stressed me out."

What do you with that??? You just can't un-ring that bell. I had to react and finish as best as possible, and at that point, that's all you can do. Things can and will go wrong. Yet, you still have to react swiftly and get the project completed with quality. I couldn't convince her, nor would I try, that we were better than her experience told her. All I could do was offer a concession and walk out the door knowing that our process let us down.

Although I was proud of our response and the finished product. The GOLD here is believing that they are NOT Cheap, Lazy, or Stupid, and that *The Customer Experience* starts from the first call and continues all the way through to the final walk-through.

When you first set out, you're going to be refining your business plan and working on your processes. If you understand your market and you're going after the right avatars and you're continually evaluating, just go out there and bumble and stumble. Try some things, make some mistakes, and calibrate your processes.

But know this: the upward trend in the request for Home Services is what's going to continue. There's an abundance of consumers who are living in single-family dwelling homes who are looking to outsource the service done on their homes. If you're a better service provider than the others, then you're going to get more of the Home Services Business in the market you're serving.

Stay away from thinking like that business owner at the beginning of this chapter, believing customers are cheap, lazy, and stupid. Make an effort to understand your customers and realize that *The Customer Experience* that you're giving them is much more important than actually fixing their air conditioner or hot water heater, or upgrading a small hall bathroom.

The 3 Secrets of the Customer
In the early years of running my business, I invested a lot of time learning and understanding the general public's mindset. I analyzed who my best customers were and what the mechanics were when I had a great transaction and everything went right for the customer. I learned and felt what operational excellence really meant and looked like … from the first customer contact to accepting their payment with a smile.

These three secrets didn't just come to me. It took roughly four years to figure them out to the point where I could share them with my team and technicians. To let them know what's really going on in the customer's mind when they call or when we arrive at the house and ring the doorbell. This allows my technicians to view themselves as equal to their customers in stature by knowing what their customers are thinking and why.

You see, in the Home Services Business, there are some customers who will immediately view their technicians as a lower class and look down their nose at them. They see a dusty physical laborer, not someone great at their craft. My intent with the three secrets was to put my technicians on the same playing field as their customers so that they could feel confident and competent and let their inner artist shine. I tell my technicians that their positive attitude also makes their customers more confident in them. The three secrets:

1. Service should be completed at the time of the transaction.
In the Home Services business, my technicians will show up ON TIME, ring the doorbell, and look prepared and ready to go with smiles on their faces. They are trained to KNOW that the customer's expectation is that the job is over as soon as they show up!

It's true. They agreed to pay you money for the service, so in their minds, the job is DONE. But you haven't done a thing yet!

So how do you overcome this incredibly impossible expectation? What do you do with the knowledge that customers expect that the job is completed the minute your technician arrives?

Well, first off, don't waste their time when you show up. They're already feeling anxious about you being there and invading their privacy. And in the COVID-19 pandemic times in which this book is being written, they're even more anxious and will be for a while to come.

Armed with this first secret, my technicians greet the customer and then in less than five minutes, walk them through the job that needs to be completed, confirm the work to be done, explain the plan to do the work, and SET the expectation that the work is NOT done yet, but they will get started immediately—all with a smile ☺.

The NOW world will only get faster. Setting expectations and EXCEEDING them will be your only path to success in this instant-gratification society in which we live, which will only accelerate. You can't hurry quality, but people will try. And you can discount speed, but people will try. Train your team on this first secret, and you'll see better results from each retail transaction.

2. People buy from people they like.

All too often, our home service technicians think that they're just there to do the service.

I tell them to be personable, smile through the phone, smile when they get there to do the work, don't get flustered if something goes wrong, and let the different customer attitudes of the anxious general public that they encounter roll off their back. We talk about creating POSITIVE energy and not trying to suck the positive out of the room.

Let me give you an example. How many times have you walked up to the register in your favorite fast-food restaurant and the person taking your order has their head down and gives you a limp and mumbly…

"How can I help you?" without even looking you in the eye.

And you respond in kind with a bland … *"I'll take a #5."*

How are you feeling about that meal and interaction? Neutral at best, but NO ENERGY!

Now walk into a Chick-fil-A (which, here in the south, is the KING of chicken sandwiches), and the young bubbly person says enthusiastically, "WELCOME TO CHICK-FIL-A… HOW CAN I SERVE YOU?" and you respond with, "#5 AND A MILKSHAKE please."

That's right! You JUST spent more than you were expecting. And you can't WAIT TO GO BACK. Their energy picks you up a little and it shows in their sales volume and customer satisfaction scores, which of course translates into a better net profit (SANITY LINE).

In the Home Services Business, your technicians are not there just to fix customer problems. They have to let their customers know, up front, that they like them, because customers want to like their technicians. And if they like your technicians, they will have a better chance of finishing the job with a flourish.

One of my best technicians used to show up to the job site and hardly make any eye contact with the customer and mumble what he was going to do. I got a call one day from a customer who said, *"Chris, I trust you buddy, but does he really know what he's doing?"*

I responded, *"Tommy knows exactly what he's doing. He's done this work at least 10 times before. I know he's got this. Don't worry."*

I thought I had taken care of the customer and the job … but OH NO! The customer was an HP mid-level executive who didn't know s**t about the work that Tommy was doing. But the executive was just used to being "that guy" who lords over people in his corporate habitat.

That customer sat there in the dining room all day with his laptop, watching Tommy work, and because the customer was constantly watching over him, he didn't get the work done. He was so nervous that he had to come back the next day to finish, and he was nervous about coming back as well! Tommy told me that although he could do the work in half the time and it was easy for him, having the customer sit there watching him was the most stressful work experience of his life.

People buy from people they like. So, show up with CONFI-DENCE to let them know that you know what you're doing. Tell them your plan and how you're going to take care of them. Tell them about how long it will take, then get busy. And do it all with a pleasant face. Teri Tennis, my ALTA mom avatar, is going to think to herself, *"Yeah, I like that guy. That guy gets a tip. That guy gets a good review. That guy gets called back to do more work."*

The bonus is that by doing a little introduction and maintaining a pleasant confident exterior, the technician will get to have a great day at work and be the artist that he wants to be. This was a lesson that Tim learned and it made him a better technician because of it.

3. People will discount a purchase by ½ the price and double the rebate offered.

Working with the general public makes the retail experience even more challenging: different personalities, different interpretations of words, and the public being generally CHRONICALLY UNIN-FORMED. Differences are the spice of life, but not managing them appropriately can cost you money.

This concept takes some explanation, but customers without any knowledge of costing, pricing, and profit will typically assume the additional product or service will cost FAR LESS than what it cost you to do it. And if they decide they don't want the product or service, they'll assume that the final price will be FAR LESS than what you'll be willing to discount the work.

To understand this further, the terms "Far," "More," "Less," and "Cheaper" are all qualitative, and when left to the discretion of the customer, they will always assume an advantage on their side. Your job is to QUANTIFY the pricing so that any price addition or reduction is fair to both parties.

The first half of this third secret is weird but true. When people accept your price, and then you get there and they change something on the work order—such as wanting you to work on one thing instead of the three things you priced the job for—they will double the amount of price reduction they're expecting in their head.

I'll give you an example. Say you contracted to do some work at a customer's home—to work on a door, fix some drywall, and fix a toilet. When you get there, the owner says to never mind fixing the one toilet, she wants you to change out two toilets instead.

The customer is going to double the price decrease in her mind for having one of the two toilets installed. Her reasoning is that you are just fixing one and thinks you can install two toilets for the price of one.

When changes to a work order are made by the customer, your technicians need to be trained to show the customer the price sheet, walk them through what's changed, and tell them what the new price is going to be. An educated consumer will understand and appreciate that, especially knowing that they're not being taken.

One of my favorite customers early on in my Home Services Business years was "Discount Dan." You might say he became an avatar. Dan was a savvy customer who lived in a gated community in a ½ million-dollar home. He was meticulous about its upkeep.

Discount Dan decided to use our services and I priced the work and he accepted. He said he would not pay my technician at the time of completion and that he would mail the payment and I agreed. I knew Dan wasn't going to stiff me. When I received payment, it included a check and two of my coupons—he decided to use the second coupon to discount the price even more.

LESSON LEARNED: "One Coupon Per Transaction" was added

to all of my advertising. Well played Discount Dan! This secret is great to share with your home services team because it helps them understand that getting agreement on pricing and scope upfront sets them up for success at the end and leaves the customer experience on a five-star level.

The Ritz Carlton Service Model

The Ritz Carlton is a premier provider of luxury-stay hotels. It is internationally known for its customer service, incredible staff, and luxury accommodations. Horst Schulze co-founded the Ritz Carlton hotel chain and was passionate about the Ritz Carlton Experience. Anybody who has come in contact with him will confirm his expectation for excellence.

I associated so deeply with Schulze's view of *The Customer Experience* that I used my experiences staying at the Ritz to form my own customer experience model. I talk about this topic a lot with my technicians during our Wednesday morning training sessions. I describe the Ritz Carlton Service Model and how it aligns with my first secret—service should be completed at the time of the transaction.

1. Customers want a product or service or output without any defects. The quality is already assumed, but the experience is more important;

2. they want to be served in a timely manner; and

3. they want the people who they're dealing with to be nice to them.

The Ritz Carlton has one huge advantage that we don't have in the Home Services Business— they get to CONTROL THEIR ENVIRONMENT. You are going THEIR place; I am coming to provide my service in YOUR CASTLE. Advantage: Ritz-Carlton.

Your customer's anxiety level is higher. They don't know what to expect because they don't know what it's going to be like to have their air conditioning off for a day or their refrigerator down for a day or have their water turned off for the day. What we need to do in the Home Services Business is to enter our customers' homes on their terms.

The way I see it, we're stepping into their castle, trying to provide a service about which they have little knowledge and no clue what to expect. Our technicians may also have to bring their own materials from a big box store or supply house, and the customer will most likely be leery of the quality of those products. When you go to a Ritz Carlton, even the chocolates have the Ritz logo on it, so of course, they're the best chocolates. Advantage Ritz Carlton.

In summary, *The Customer Experience* in home services is filled with as many variables as there are customers. Embrace their craziness, learn to live with and within their world, and arrive with their expectations in mind.

5

Aiming for Operational Excellence

We are what we repeatedly do.
Excellence, then, is not an act but a habit.

—Aristotle

You've jumped!

You're starting your journey. You're out there in the wild and you're running by yourself with your funding, with your great idea, and with your finger on the pulse of your avatars. Most importantly, you know the importance of *The Customer Experience*.

Now you're going to learn what delivery looks like and what making a successful company really takes.

I started by figuring out who my best customers were. And when we had a great transaction and the customer loved us and everything went right, I learned what operational excellence looked like. We locked the pathway to those transactions into our memories! I also learned who my worst customers were and where my operationally processes failed.

I was out to make my millions at $80/hour per home services visit. I was moving forward— yes, little by little and inch by inch, but I WAS MOVING FORWARD!

The Flywheel Effect

It may feel like you're pushing against a great weight each day, but believe me, eventually the momentum will begin to work in your favor.

In his book, *Good to Great*, Jim Collins refers to that momentum as, "The Flywheel Effect,"[8] and that's exactly what happened for my company. The effect illustrates that *Good to Great* transformations never happen in one fell swoop or as a result of some new process, or a killer innovation, or just a lucky break. Rather, it's the result of a relentless pushing of a great flywheel, turn upon turn, building momentum; in my case, at $80/hour a turn working on people's homes.

After you start getting up each day and going out to people's homes to make it happen, the momentum will start to work in your favor, and you'll be pushing no harder than you were in your early months. Then each turn of the flywheel will build upon the work done earlier, compounding your investment of effort.

It takes personal and professional habits to succeed. Putting on my shirt with The Trusted Toolbox company logo and a pair of clean khaki pants, having a smile on my face, and delivering on *The Customer Experience* showed my purpose to my customers and my team each and every day.

And as you start to scale—which essentially assumes you'll need more people—you'll want your habits known and adopted by each person on the day they're hired. Going forward, you'll seek out those people who will have those same values and habits that you do.

> ***The people you want working for you are the ones***
> ***who want to be their best.***

From my company's infancy to its adolescence to where I am today as a growing enterprise, my values and habits have become the culture of the company. This consistent daily approach led to my overnight success, just 12 years in the making! I still wear the uniform each day. It's a small thing, but it reinforces my expectation of customer service excellence. The occasional day that I come in without my red logo shirt and khaki pants, I'll get a comment as sure as the sun rises. *"Chris, I didn't know it was an Out of uniform day?"*

I LOVE IT! That's GOLD. My team knows what I expect when it comes to the uniform.

You have to live your habits each day and help your people build their competence and confidence in those habits. They have to believe it's going to make their lives better. The more confident my technicians are, the better they are at their craft, and the more competent they become. And it builds upon itself like a flywheel and the momentum starts to happen. And then the money starts to happen. And my people's personal and professional objectives start to become realized.

The Trusted Toolbox - Flywheel Effect

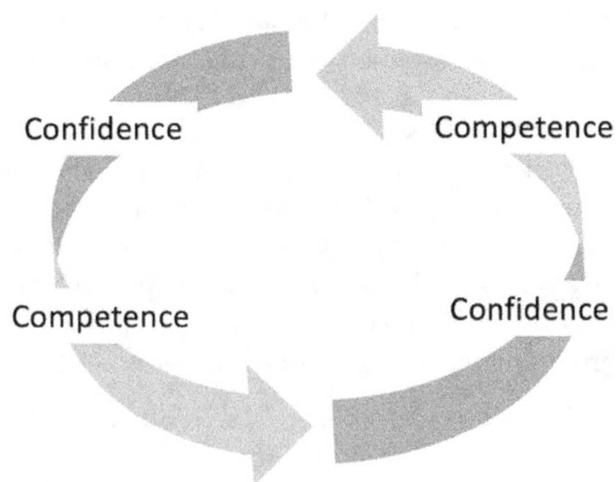

The GOLD HERE is found in each turn of the Flywheel: Confidence building Competence building Confidence building Competence. Consistent, mindful attempts to deliver *The Customer Experience* rotate the wheel and build MOMENTUM, and you can't stop momentum.

Habits for the Wild

As Aristotle once said, "Excellence is not an act, but a habit." And if you get the right habits in place and your team follows your habits, Operational Excellence will follow.

How do you start your day?

When I'm working at my highest and best, I check my to-do list, check my calendar and what I'm trying to accomplish for the week, and then get back to focusing on today and driving for operational excellence. Gone, by the way, were the 40 hours of corporate zoo meetings—every week!

When my day is going the wrong way, the first thing I do is look at my phone and check for emails and text messages, react to customers whims, and let the distractions deter from my goals and turning the flywheel.

When I am at my best, I fall into the habits that help: I work out in the morning; I get my uniform on; and I tackle the day looking to maximize my Return on Effort (ROE).

Unless its Monday. Mondays in the Home Services Business are usually a series of curveballs and knuckleballs, and then a fastball right between the eyes, and you have to be able to react quickly, use your processes, and get back to your goal of ROE to keep moving forward. I never make large decisions on Mondays and typically don't schedule any meetings so that I can react to what Mondays bring. Sometimes I get pleasantly surprised and nothing earth shattering happens.

Check Some F*****G Boxes

If you don't have Time Management as a success habit packed away, GET IT. I have developed a system that works for me because it allows me to take care of daily items, plan out the week with activities that line up with my yearly goals, and increase my ROE. My time management system became a fusion of white-collar and blue-collar philosophies—a hybrid of Steven Covey and a builder I met years ago.

*The fusion of the two resulted in "CHECK Some F*****G Boxes" as my mantra.*

Stephen Covey's, *The Seven Habits of Highly Effective People*, was introduced to me in my first engineering job and it helped me focus on completing assignments and making sure they were accurate. The reason I bought the book? It was my first job and I was a young, cocky engineer with a master's degree who thought he was the smartest guy in the room (which got beat out of me pretty quickly... but that's a different story).

I had been there three months and felt like I was taking care of business until my manager, George Hays, came up to me and pulled me aside. Now George was the quintessential engineer (think Dilbert comic strip), and I was the young cocky engineer ... I thought it was RAISE TIME or PROMOTION TIME. Maybe he wanted me to run the company? ... NOPE.

Instead, he said ...

> *"Chris, I have no doubt that you know what you're doing and I do think you'll not only be my boss, but will run this company, but for GOD'S SAKE, can you stay focused on a task and get things completed?"*

As I got into my car that night to head home, I realized that he was RIGHT. I drove to the bookstore, bought *The Seven Habits of Highly Effective People*, ordered the Franklin Planner, and started to work on my Habits. It was great advice from George that I've never forgotten since. He believed in me and gave me constructive advice and I respected him for that and for many other things. I ended up getting promoted and then left the company. But those habits learned in the zoo have since helped me in the wild.

The second iteration in my time management evolution came several years later when I was working as a consultant and my wife and I were building our house on the lake. We found a place that was being built as a "spec home," a custom home under construction with the hope that someone would buy it close to or just after it was completed. We went ahead and contracted to buy the house with some modifications.

The builder's construction superintendent's name was Charlie. When I met him, I could tell he knew his craft and was incredibly organized with materials and processes for managing sub-contractors and customer requests. One day when Charlie had his folder out, I noticed an interesting to-do checklist. I asked him to explain his system.

He said he would write down the task on the right side and who he either needed information from to complete the "To-Do" or who was assigned to complete it. He then drew an empty box to the left of the task.

When the task got started, he would fill in ½ of the box with his pen to visually let him know that action had started or the to-do was "in play." When it was completed, he CHECKED THE BOX. Charlie was extremely efficient with his checklist-driven approach to home building. And I quickly blended Charlie's method in with my Stephen Covey system.

I met Charlie at the job site one day and I could hear a heated exchange between him and a subcontractor. I let them finish their discussion and then walked into the house. I said, *"Hey Charlie, how's it going?"*

Charlie replied, *"It's a Monday, but that's not going to stop me."*

Then he looked at me and said, *"Sometimes you got to checking some F*****G Boxes, whether somebody wants you to or not."*

I've since used my system in the corporate zoo and in the wild. I've moved back and forth between paper and electronic forms, but my habit on Monday mornings is to go into my electronic form for the current week, see what items are not checked, and then get in my truck and set out to get the boxes checked.

Here is an outline of my format as a visual.

<table>
<tr><td colspan="3">Chris's To Do List<td align="right"><u>MM/DD/YYYY</u></td></tr>
<tr><td>Primaries</td><td>Follow-ups</td><td>Longer-Term Goals</td></tr>
<tr><td>☐ ____</td><td>☐ ____</td><td>☐ ____</td></tr>
<tr><td>☐ ____</td><td>☐ ____</td><td>☐ ____</td></tr>
<tr><td>☐ ____</td><td>☐ ____</td><td>☐ ____</td></tr>
<tr><td>☐ ____</td><td>☐ ____</td><td>☐ ____</td></tr>
<tr><td>Loose Ends</td><td>1-1's</td><td>Personal</td></tr>
<tr><td>☐ ____</td><td>☐ ____</td><td>☐ ____</td></tr>
<tr><td>☐ ____</td><td>☐ ____</td><td>☐ ____</td></tr>
<tr><td>☐ ____</td><td>☐ ____</td><td>☐ ____</td></tr>
<tr><td>☐ ____</td><td>☐ ____</td><td>☐ ____</td></tr>
</table>

Time management is a discipline that we all fall in and out of in terms of doing it well. In the corporate zoo, if you're off your game a little that day and you don't feel like checking boxes, you can find a corner and hide for a while. But if you try to hide from your business, and don't stay in the discipline of good habits, you'll certainly be ONE of the NINE-OUT-OF-TEN who fails.

I start my day with the To-Do list from the day before, and I don't let the urgent activities take precedent over the important activities (Covey talk). But sometimes it is just easier to take care of the urgent, simple stuff and take a mental break from the harder, more important activities. It can happen, and I just embrace it and reapproach the important thinking activities a little later in the day.

Coming to Terms with Myself

In his book, *The E-Myth: Revisited: Why Most Small Businesses Don't Work and What to Do About It,* author Michael Gerber walks you through the steps in the life of a business—from entrepreneurial infancy through adolescent growing pains to the mature entrepreneurial perspective: the guiding light of all businesses that succeed—and shows how to apply the lessons of franchising to any business, whether or not it's a franchise.[9]

Most importantly, he draws the distinction between working ON your business and working IN your business. I also connected with Gerber's view that the entrepreneur needs to be three people:

1. the ENTREPRENEUR with the big picture, knowing where you're going to go,

2.   the MANAGER, who manages the operations, and

3.   the TECHNICIAN, who is good at tasks.

Great book, but man, those three hats couldn't be more diametrically opposed!

It was frustrating for me to constantly try to figure out when I would need to put on my entrepreneur hat or my manager hat. And then, at a moment's notice, put on my technician hat and go out there in the field and fix something at a customer's house. Now, I wasn't the best technician, but I was a very good manager, and that was a hat that I had a hard time letting go of because I enjoyed it and it came natural to me.

Yet, it was still frustrating when I was hiring, training, and managing people. I couldn't be the ENTREPRENEUR, planning my next moves for my multimillion-dollar handyman business at $80/hour per visit. Worse yet, it's hard to think about the business when you're out there balancing on a ladder, installing a window.

I definitely wanted my time to be a whole lot more entrepreneurial than having to deal with manager issues or being out in the field trying to pass as a technician. I began to realize that my job was to let my processes work and manage and perfect those processes.

The inflection point was my coming to terms with myself. I HAD TO LEARN TO LET GO. But it was hard letting go early on. I didn't know if I had the right processes in place. Right around that time, a string of customer issues happened in succession that made me begin to worry about the quality of our work.

REDOs

While I developed processes to make sure that my guys were successful in completing their jobs, what I didn't do was develop and design all the processes to make sure that we didn't have "REDOs."

What's a redo in the Home Services Business?

In short, it's an expensive lesson to learn. You're probably thinking it's when you have to go back and redo something that you did wrong or complete something that wasn't completed, such as redoing some drywall, or re-hanging the door, or tightening up the plumbing under the kitchen sink. It costs money to go back for new materials or additional labor, AND there's the opportunity cost because you're not out getting your next job completed, laying you a BIG OLD ZERO NEW REVENUE GOOSE EGG.

I discovered that a REDO in the Home Services Business meant that we didn't completely meet the customer's expectations. After being in business for two years, I had five redo calls in one day from five different customers. Five situations where we had to go back and REDO something. I mean, FIVE REDOs in one day … I only had four technicians!

I thought to myself, *"Oh my God! This is an avalanche. WE MUST SUCK!"*

The words that I heard years ago in the corporate zoo—when I was running loan operations for a commercial loans sales manager who was not impressed with my organization's delivery—came ringing back … *"It's always easier to ASK for good service than PROVIDE it."*

Truer words have never been spoken. I thought to myself that we don't even know what quality is. Then I stopped beating myself up for a minute in order to assess the REDOs:

- The first REDO was a callback because we missed a piece of trim.

- The second was a customer calling us to finish cleaning up after the job.

- The third REDO was a call from a customer saying that the technician was taking too long and she had to ask him to leave.

- … And it just kept on coming.

When I realized I had a problem, I shut the business down that Thursday and told all my guys to come back on Monday. I put on my toolbelt and I went out to start investigating each of the REDOs.

The 1ˢᵗ REDO: involved my technician missing a piece of trim. Now, what you should know is that in every Home Services Business, the PROFIT of the job is established THE MOMENT THE ESTIMATE IS GIVEN. That's GOLD. So, in this case, I did the estimate on this job where we had missed a piece of trim.

When I looked at my technician's work order, that piece of trim wasn't part of his scope of work; it wasn't on the work order. So, my estimator (ME!) had missed something that the customer expected. I went out and bought the trim piece, came back, got in a hurry, cut it wrong, RECUT IT, caulked, painted, and finished, and got paid. So much for the GOLD. The bear ate me on this one!

The 2ⁿᵈ REDO: involved my technician not cleaning up after the job was completed. When I showed up, the customer started to explain, *"I didn't want to tell your guy about the trash because I was concerned there would be a confrontation."*

I told the customer, *"No problem! I'll go ahead and clean up everything right now."*

I pulled my truck around to get the trash, and found that the customer had added to the pile with some household items. I collected payment for the work and headed off to the third REDO. So far, in both the first and second cases, the quality of the work being done by my technicians was perfect. So, we didn't suck at that, which was very heartening!

The 3ʳᵈ REDO: When I arrived at the customer's house, she immediately cited the work that was NOT completed. She laid out the timeline of events that started with my technician showing up 1 ½ hours late without calling to inform her that he was going to be late. She said he then had to get supplies, which took two hours, according to the customer, and seemed in a hurry to finish.

She saved the real issue until the end. He was there at dinner time, and she wanted him out of the house and not interfering with her family before or during dinner. After I listened to the story, I grabbed my toolbelt, put in two pieces of baseboard, tested the sink vanity for plumbing, and collected. He was one hour away from finishing.

It wasn't poor quality of work that caused the rash of REDOs. Instead, there was work left to be done in all three instances.

I realized that my processes and procedures didn't tell my guys what needed to be done, when it needed to be done, and how they needed to finish. And I didn't convey strong enough that *The Customer Experience* was more important than the work that they were doing.

Shutting my business down for four days gave me time.

Coming out of this epiphany, I came up with three new tasks within a simple framework that would help them deliver on *The Customer Experience* so they could go out there and be successful every day. These three simple activities that I added to our process align with the Three Secrets of the Customer shared in Chapter 3 and reflect our habits at The Trusted Toolbox. My people know that these are non-negotiable activities that must be done:

1. Call your customer 30 minutes ahead of your appointment time— NO MATTER WHAT.

2. Have the customer review and sign the work order BEFORE beginning work.

3. Have the customer review the work and sign the work order at the END to signify they approve of the work.

The GOLD in this is a continuous assessment of what's going wrong and right and realizing that small changes can make HUGE differences.

Negotiation and Conflict Resolution

Solving a conflict through communication and negotiation is inevitable in the Home Services Business, and being able to recognize when you have a conflict to resolve is important. The way you react and respond will determine the quality of both *The Customer Experience* and your company's ultimate profitability.

We once worked on an "ex-friend" of mine's bathroom and it didn't go well at all. I got the call from him that started with, *"Hey buddy, things aren't going well, can you come over and take a look at where we are and see what we can do to get this bathroom finished?"*

The conflict worked its way into a death spiral the moment I asked if we could stay on it and finish the job, and he agreed. When it was time to present the final bill, I asked for $7,000.00 more to complete the job, with the intent of splitting the difference between what I actually thought the job was worth and trying to cover my true costs. I was trying to do the right thing.

As a side note, if you saw the work we performed, you would argue that the quality was excellent and worth the final invoice. If you objectively looked at the timeline and cluster of errors though, you would probably argue that it wasn't really worth it. There were two sides to this story, but my intent was to try to Negotiate a Conflict.

I went into the final discussion prepared for each of the Best, Expected, and Worst Outcome Scenarios. I knew it was going to be a very difficult discussion. He and his wife had just returned from vacation. We had completed the actual work three weeks before. And they were already using the master bathroom. I got the WORST outcome.

My ex-friend said, *"Hey buddy, I want to make sure we're still friends, but I don't think I owe you any more money. You and I can agree that this was a BAD experience and your guys were just incompetent. So, what do you say?"*

I was blown away! I didn't know how to respond and I really CHOKED on the response. I was about to lose $4,000.00 in labor and material costs.

I had a list of things that I failed to remind him of: that he and his wife caused the last two months of delays by standing us up at the house; by refusing us entrance into the house; by calling out false issues; and by creating chaos by bringing in their own tile guy to finish work that they felt wasn't done correctly.

At that time, I didn't have the discipline nor the fortitude to argue the correct points and save myself from losing $4,000. This was a tough pill to swallow for a home service professional and needless to say, I lost a friend. Additionally, I poured a lot of personal time capital into that project and in addition to losing the money, the opportunity cost was enormous.

What did I learn from that transaction?

Two things:
1. Don't become too passionate and make things personal. Find ways to step back and be more objective.

2. Know when to cut your losses; know when to walk away. I was NEVER going to make this type of customer happy.

When I first got that call from that customer, I didn't react with the firepower necessary to get us out of there. I let him dictate the timeline. And I let my guys talk me into a slow and steady completion, when an all-hands-on-deck team-approach would have ultimately saved my money and time.

Finally, I learned to exit with as much grace and dignity as I can. I was NOT going to make them happy; they were NOT going to pay me the additional costs. I let it become personal and did NOT make the correct business or personal decisions.

In negotiation and conflict resolution, you'll always need to balance your passion and drive with compassion and detachment. You need to be prepared for three possible outcomes: Best, Expected, and Worst. I've always made great decisions when I'm mindful of these three likely outcomes. Of course, you'll drive for the best outcome for you or your business, but you need to stay detached enough to not let your passion and drive take over and lead you down a path that may end up creating a WORST outcome.

The GOLD is keeping detached enough to recognize the conflict and work to resolve it swiftly so that you can move on and spend your time on customers who appreciate what you do and pay you for your great customer service.

I took all of these lessons learned and GOLD nuggets banked and I implemented more processes and hired good people to help me run the business. We started to hit our stride! Our Flywheel was picking up speed. I didn't get into the negotiations or conflicts any longer—at least not immediately anymore.

I started to get great feedback on our delivery and our customer experience. I was able to start moving to the next level in my business and was able to reconnect with my mentors and share my next-level thoughts. I was feeling really strong about my business and its potential.

Already in a Rut?!

I was getting to that phase where I was aiming for operational excellence every day and I thought I was there. I had pulled up to a position where I didn't have to solve every problem—every estimate was being handled by someone on my team, every customer issue that came up was being taken care of by someone on my team who understood *The Customer Experience*, and the customer's bills were being issued and collected.

I was able to start working and becoming more of the Entrepreneurial leader and less of the Manager and almost nothing of the Technician (that last one to the benefit of my customers ☺).

I was on the cusp of success. I had a chance to go back and review my business plan and meet with the mentors I had established when I first set out. I was able to take them back through where I started and ask them those same precise questions that I had asked of them early on. It was in this reconnecting that a mentor showed me a huge GOLD nugget where I didn't expect to find one.

I remember telling him how great things were going—that I found a great operations manager and two good salespeople and how I was able to work *ON* my business. He started asking me some really pointed questions and I gave him direct and honest answers. And then he asked, *"How is your net profit?"*

I answered with my topline (VANITY LINE) and then told him my net profit (SANITY LINE), and as I talked, he sat there and listened, and then said,

"Chris, you're in a rut, man!"

I was sort of stunned, honestly, and caught flatfooted. We talked for a while longer and then I got into my truck and drove back to the office. How could he say that? Since we had last met, I had improved my net profit by two percent and my topline by five percent. Thirty-five minutes later—the time it took to drive home—I realized that he was right. I was in a rut. I was on cruise control. I wasn't paying attention to my SANITY LINE.

I wasn't constantly on the hunt for continuous improvement. My company boat was rising with everyone else's, but I was rising at the same pace as everyone else. I wasn't outpacing them. I went back to my office and played back in my mind another comment he made,

"For that amount of revenue, you should expect DOUBLE your current NET PROFIT, or maybe the juice just isn't worth the squeeze."

UGGGH, he was right.

I was smart making a go of it in the wild. I was hard-working. I had my success goals in place and they were not all monetary. But being "worth the squeeze" was an important point to reflect on. You see, I had just gotten done telling my wife,

"Oh, we're right on the cusp! Next year is going to be the breakout year!"

So, I internalized the crisis, put the pressure on myself, went back to checking boxes, and looked again at what I really wanted to be when I grew up and how I could achieve Operational Excellence.

6

Achieving Operational Excellence

"We cannot solve our problems with the same thinking that we used when created them.

—Albert Einstein

in·flec·tion point

noun

1. *Mathematics*: a point at which a change in the direction of curvature occurs.

2. *Business*: a time of significant change in a situation; a turning point.

After hearing, *"Chris, you're in a rut, man,"* I set aside the weekend to take stock and do a reality check with myself to see if I had just wasted eight years. So, I did. I went back to basics, pulled out the business plan, and reviewed my financials and other key performance indicators.

I realized I hadn't updated my five-year business plan in almost four years. I started by analyzing where we were performing well as a company and where we needed to make improvements.

I had three completely different new business owners suggest that I look into the *Entrepreneurial Operating* System (EOS), by Gino Wickman, as a model for creating more ownership and buy-in by everyone within my company.[10]

I researched EOS and ended up buying Wickman's book, *Traction: Get a Grip on Your Business,* where, within an Entrepreneurial Operating System, you can begin strengthening the six key components of your business: (1) vision, (2) people, (3) data, (4) issues, (5) process, and (5) traction.[11]

You could tell that these three business owners had adopted the EOS by their questions:

"Dude, where's your five-year, three-year, and one-year plans?"

> *"Chris, where's your 'painted picture' so your guys know
> where they're going?"*

I used Wickman's book as a blueprint. It's a very detailed, action-biased book. I liked Wickman's six areas of focus, which inspired me to take action on the six biggest things that I had to work on.

I was all in after hearing about the discipline of structuring the business plan in five-, three-, and one-year milestones; having it documented; and getting my people to share in my vision. This new level of discipline really helped me script my plans and document all my processes. This would set The Trusted Toolbox up for its next level of growth.

I saw it as an inflection point for the company and I zeroed in on the opportunities that I would need to tackle in order to lift me out of the rut I was in. I distilled it down to these six:

1st … I had a mission statement—but I was the only person who knew it by heart.

2nd … I had procedures and processes—but they were sparsely documented.

3rd … My software and technology infrastructure were being maintained by ME.

4th … I needed to know my Key Performance Indicators (KPIs).

5th … My reputation online was good, but we had only 80 reviews after eight years.

6th … My team didn't know my 5/3/1-year goals.

You know I love to solve problems, so here's what I discovered and resolved in each…

1st … Only I knew the Mission Statement

I've had experience with mission statements in the past in corporate America with my own teams, but I soon realized that the process of creating and implanting a mission statement with a professional white-collar organization didn't translate to the blue-collar world. And why is that?

I think it's because the blue-collar world sees mission statements as just words and not values—words and not actions. I've heard consultants say that you should recite your mission statement before each meeting. Sorry, but that doesn't work with my wolfpack.

The first thing I realized was that I wasn't translating the mission statement into something everyone could experience and remember. And if it wasn't being understood correctly, it most likely wasn't being executed at the customer level as well I had thought.

In my corporate zoo years, I worked in two different organizations where, as the leader, I co-wrote the mission statements and defined the culture of the team. I was the active ingredient that made sure that each organization was focused on the right activities and always rose to the occasion in doing the right things for our customers.

I drove the teams in each organization to think about each and every word on their mission statement, so I had to make it brief and easy to remember. If too wordy, nobody was going to read it, believe it, or embrace it as their purpose too, and not just my purpose or the company's purpose.

Learning from my experience, I developed the mission statement for The Trusted Toolbox, being careful to craft a short, memorable declaration that spoke to everyone.

**THE TRUSTED TOOLBOX
MISSION STATEMENT**

Putting Customers 1st by delivering professional home repair
services that build trust while completing quality home repairs
and renovations using our core principles of:
Integrity, Dependability, Competence in Our Craft,
Confidence in Our Abilities, and Clear Communication.

The following Wednesday morning at our weekly training session, I asked if anyone knew our mission statement. They couldn't remember A SINGLE WORD!

I learned that in the blue-collar service world, mission statements fall flat. Real flat. In this world, people don't rally around "statements" like they do in the corporate world. They don't resonate with our people. The GOLD here for me was discovering a better, more memorable way of getting my direction out to everyone. What I did differently was invest $1,000 dollars in a **Mission Plaque** that everyone could see when they entered the training room. We reinforced its message through bonus incentive programs. And the words began to ring with my wolfpack.

Once I translated the mission statement to the Mission Plaque and reinforced the meanings repetitively, we started to pick up traction in our ability to train around those values. All the employees began to connect with what was expected.

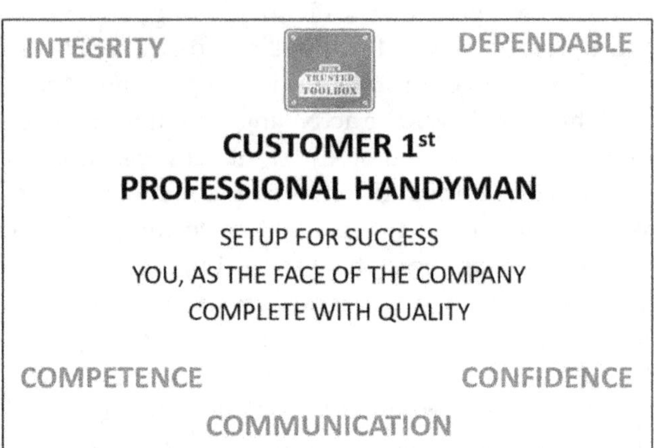

I knew it was resonating because on any given day, a team member would return to the office and give examples of "putting the customer first." the Mission Plaque helped move the culture by getting what I was thinking and believing into something that could be understood by everyone in the organization.

At that time, I had grown to 15 people, and when I couldn't be everywhere at the same time, my message needed to be living and present and top of mind with everyone each and every day. I needed to get them all to understand the direction and purpose of The Trusted Toolbox and their role in the company's success—and their success! The Mission Plaque turned out to be the vehicle and a great visual upon which to build. Yet, there were other things that didn't translate very well with my people.

"What Does Excellent Customer Service Looks Like?"
For the past year, I had talked about the Ritz Carlton Experience during our training sessions and how our CUSTOMER EXPERIENCE was striving to be like the Ritz Carlton model. In one of our sessions, I needed to see if I was breaking through in conveying over the months what excellent customer service looked like, so I asked …

"How many of you have stayed at the Ritz Carlton?"

ZERO! No one raised their hands.

I then asked, *"How many know what the Ritz Carlton is?"*

A quarter of them knew it was a hotel. That meant that 75 percent, the majority of my team, had no idea what I was comparing us to!

I realized that I needed to start using examples they could immediately connect with and comprehend like QuikTrip convenience stores. These stores were a retail outfit that my wolfpack experienced each and every day in the Atlanta area. Where they got the same great, fast, convenient, friendly service each and every time, whether for gas, breakfast, or lunch.

The combination of our Mission Plaque reinforced with the mentions of great customer service organizations during our training sessions helped move us and keep us out of the rut.

2nd ... My Procedures and Processes Were Barely Documented

My passion and hands-on approach interacting with everyone each day worked well when we were a smaller outfit, but it was time to get everyone rowing in the same direction without my having to be present all of the time.

It was time to produce a documented *The Trusted Toolbox Operations Manual.* But just as with the business plan, I wasn't shooting for getting an "A" from my professor or spending the weekend polishing a turd for someone back at zoo headquarters. I went after it, hitting all the key components, as you can see in the Table of Contents, and really using it to document what my people needed to do to shine.

The Trusted Toolbox
Operations Manual

Table of Contents:

1. Functional Organization Chart
2. HR Process
3. Customer Service Process
4. Sales and Estimator Processes
5. Operations Daily Processes
6. Operations Monthly Processes
7. Training Plans
8. Marketing and Advertising Plans
9. Financial Processes
10. Reporting
11. Physical Office Layout
12. Records Management
13. Call Scripts
14. Technology Blueprint
15. General Business Considerations
16. Project Management
17. Drafts
18. Management Reporting Framework

I learned that having them help me develop the components of the manual allowed us all to better communicate with the people I was hiring and adding to the team. The existing team was able to move with my Quick Pivots, but a lot was getting lost in translation for the new people who were waiting for me to give them direction. And here I thought they were all getting it!

NOT TRUE. I learned that I needed to start typing my requests to my people. That was the GOLD: slowing down, documenting everything important, and telling them where they were headed. I was amazed at the progress. They saw my focus and passion for our team and they got behind creating and using our new Operations Manual.

I scripted my new hire processes, my termination processes, and all of our technician training. We also designed and documented a

10-step sales process that we continually train on and expect our sales team to follow.

Respect the Individual

The documentation process took me back to one of the first jobs I ever had—in a machine shop—where I thought I was the young, know-it-all hot shot. They put me on a production machine where my task each day was to take a blank piece of metal on my left side, put it in the machine, push two buttons, take the piece out, and put it on my right side … and repeat that process … eight hours a day.

I remember working on that machine day in and day out, thinking this was SO beneath me. I was a smart guy; I was a high achiever in high school and on my way to college. I was having a hard time believing I was doing menial work. Then one day, the guy next to me started up a conversation. And I discovered that he had just gotten out of prison, never graduated high school, and had four children—each out of wedlock.

Here emerged my "Judgy McJudgy": I thought, *"You poor guy. You need to be like me!"*

Now, the way we were assessed working at the machine shop was based on how many parts we produced and how many of those parts passed an independent quality inspection. At the end of that week, the ex-prisoner, father of four had not only doubled my output in production of parts, but ALL of his parts passed inspection. And here I was—this smartass know-it-all—pumping out only a little more than half of his production each week, and half of my parts were sent back to me because they were "out of spec." I had to go back and sort those parts out on my own time and get them correctly run … ON MY TIME.

I learned not to judge others who, with direction and coaching, can take a task and complete it to perfection. It's fine if you're not that person. But those folks are needed in the workplace, especially in the Home Services Business. Each and every day, people are calling us, asking us questions, and looking for good service. That realization was GOLD for me, and that person doing his level best each day with all the challenges in his life taught me to never judge anyone and to Respect the Individual.

One of the more valuable tools in the manual was designed to helped my team understand the customer's buying process and how to nurture a best outcome with new leads and repeat customers. It opened their eyes to how customers are trying to work through, in their own mind and process, if, when, and how they're going to work with our company.

The Customer Track

In the Home Services Business, people call us because something's broken that needs fixing, or they want to upgrade or enhance a certain part of their home, or accommodate a lifestyle change. They research their options and will contact The Trusted Toolbox as part of their research and decision-making process.

Graphics can be very instrumental in conveying ideas to people. So, I created The Customer Track graphic for my inside team, to portray the customer's thinking process and help them understand their role in the customer's reasoning and buying process.

The Customer Track

Life	Situation What are they thinking?	Options	Research	Contact	Buy
	Break/Fix - wood rot - leak - drywall - etc. Enhancements: - new fixture - bathroom - remodel Lifestyle: - accommodate a pet - convert a room - aging in place Commercial	- Fix Yourself - Do Nothing - Handyman - Painter - Remodeler - 'Friend'	- Friend - Internet - Google - Review Sites - Angie's list - Trust Dale - BBB - Community Group - Call Handyman - Call Remodeler	Decision made Contact 1, 2, or 3	Check 'Hope'

Advertising

Relational / Transactional

The Customer Track is structured around the premise that 95 percent of my target market at any point in time is not in need of home services. LIFE goes on and then one day, a SITUATION happens in the house that requires their attention and some action to be taken.

They need to explore their OPTIONS, do some RESEARCH, then CONTACT the service provider or supplier, and ultimately make a decision and a purchase. Now, we all HOPE that the need arises and they buy right away at our retail price—but that's the HOPE track. Let's take a *hypothetical example.*

LIFE is simply happening for Mr. Smith. Then one morning in early November, he learns from his wife that her parents are coming for Thanksgiving. He immediately (and vividly) remembers how his mother-in-law commented last Thanksgiving—in front of everyone—on the hole in the wall in the living room. Mr. Smith now has a SITUATION. He needs to assess his OPTIONS:

Option #1: Not fix it and have his mother-in-law tell his wife and the entire family how lazy he is (Remember, this is all *hypothetical and definitely not me* ☺),

Option #2: Fix it himself, or

Option #3: Hire someone.

Mr. Smith does his research and decides it would be best to hire someone to do it. He then contacts a handyman company and has the hole in the wall fixed. Thanksgiving is a huge success, until his mother-in-law mentions in front of everyone that the toilet is running.

The Customer Track was originally developed to help dial in my marketing and figure out where to spend advertising dollars most effectively. It was also intended to help my sales guys understand the mindset of the customer and what they were walking into each day when they were in the customer's home.

Then it dawned on me that everyone involved in *The Customer Experience* needed to know about The Customer Track so they too could see how their role fit into the bigger piece of the puzzle.

Whether it was the ladies answering the phones and fielding inquiries, the estimator trying to close the deal, the scheduler trying to schedule the technicians and accommodate the customer's needs, or our technicians trying to complete the job, everyone needed to know how they fit into the customer's reasoning and buying process.

3rd ... *I* Was Our IT Department

Technology is great, until it doesn't work! Guess what can't happen when your phones go to a fast-busy signal in the retail world. Guess what happens when you can't get emails or webform submissions from people who would like to inquire about your services. People will assume you're out of business and move on. Now there's a sure-fire way to be ONE of the NINE-OUT-OF-TEN who fails for not staying on top of their equipment. Technology is necessary for almost all companies to succeed, and when it breaks, chaos can and will ensue.

Back in the corporate zoo, I was used to walking out to my assistant and asking her to get someone to fix ALL of my computer issues, even the simplest technology tasks. When you're in the corporate environment, all you need to do is just show up and get your work done, and the IT department will take care of all your technology needs.

When I first started my company, I had to learn to set up computers, get software to work, and figure out what it meant when people said, "THE INTERNET AIN'T WORKING!" I was skilled with computers, so doing the early IT work fit into my SOLD (Strengths, Opportunity, Likes, Dislikes) Framework.

Throughout our early growth, I set up people's computers and troubleshot what needed to be fixed. The tipping point for me was that every day at 3:00PM, for about a month, our computers would start slowing down. I would often walk into the office after having been out in the field to find one person out back smoking a cigarette, one on their personal phone, and one threatening to quit because they couldn't get anything done. After a lot of head scratching and assessing, I was able to determine that our server had run out of memory.

It was time to get an IT firm to help so we could get back to work and stay working all day long. Your ultimate technology need is a hard one to manage and predict. I've made a number of 'pain point' decisions and have also waited a little too long to make the change to improve our performance. After making the move to hire an outside IT firm to help us, our 3pm smoke and phone breaks were gone and everyone was happy to have faster working computers.

My suggestion here is to have as MINIMAL a technology blueprint and as little dependency on technology as possible. Resist the urge to buy and build the best and the biggest technology platform without seeing where your company is heading.

This IT firm helped us with our technical health and to always be OPEN for business. Our processes began to run better because my people had phones that worked and computers that moved faster … LIFE WAS GOOD! It costs money to solve problems, and I remembered the net profit over time graph, but I knew that if I was going to get out of this rut, I needed to make the technology investment.

It was expensive resolving my major technology hardware pain, but nothing compares to the mental pain of having to change software.

Don't Buy the Ferrari
Changing software is PAINFUL! Ask any business owner who's done it and they'll tell you that the change is enough to make you

want to chuck your PC right up against a wall (yep … did that too!).

I started my business with the belief that there was no way I could provide great operational excellence without some kind of a CRM (Customer Relationship Management) system. At the time, there were off-the-shelf CRM software packages, but nothing cloud-based, as they are today. Nevertheless, I picked a simple software package on the lower end of the price scale so it wouldn't break the bank and could grow with me.

The GOLD nugget here is don't buy the Ferrari when you only need a work truck. A Ferrari CRM would have been a total waste of time and money. Why? Because I wasn't ready to work with a robust CRM system and needed to save a few $$$ in the startup.

Once we started using the software, my two remote sales estimators and five internal people said that the CRM system wasn't helping them get their work done. The greatest frustration for my sales team was the software's inability to be used remotely.

Without access to the Internet, I couldn't see anything when I was in the field, and I needed to because I was out selling and needed to access my company's data. Today, virtually everything is cloud based so we made the switch to a web-based cloud system, which allows us better access to information and quicker responses to customer requests.

This GOLD is in making sure you have a good handle on your processes before making the software switch. Have your processes documented so your new software provider will better understand your requirements. Documentation also serves you and the service provider as a contract with expectations and specifications if features and capabilities are missing.

I chose a cloud-based software package that was somewhat customizable. This meant we had to convert our existing customer base to the new software platform and learn how to use the new system. What added to the challenge was that the IT team who developed the software were all remote. On top of that, they were originally from Russia, now living in Canada. I had to learn to talk another language in addition to stumbling over the IT language in order to explain our requirements and processes.

I learned to speak Canadian-Russian-IT all rolled into one. I called it "CaRusIT" when I would get frustrated and say, *"What did he mean to say?"* or *"What the hell is this, I didn't want the system to do that!"*

The change we underwent to a new software system made us

faster and more able to manage our growing team. It will also be able to scale with us for five more years based on my growth plans. My software vendor did well, and as long as I have my CaRusIT-to-English dictionary handy, we'll continue to have good upgrades, enhancements, and resolutions.

4th ... Measuring the Right Things—KPIs (Key Performance Indicators)

Peter Drucker famously said, *"What gets measured gets improved."*

So, let's measure everything ... ☺ ... but, that doesn't work so well.

What does work is centering your attention first on those metrics that will quantify specific areas of importance. It's vital to get a handle on what to measure and at what frequency early in your process and then watch them regularly. These are the metrics I frequently use:

Sales Lead Tracking—I use several metrics in this important area: How many leads came in per week; where did they come from; what was the LEAD SOURCE; and were they LEADS that we could actually convert and deliver?

A valuable statistic that we keep track of is NET LEADS. It tracks how many true opportunities we have in winning someone's business. We then subtract out those leads that we can't service due to scope, location, or timeliness. Knowing the number of Sales Leads is good. But knowing NET Leads is even more powerful and telling. Why?

1. It tells us how many REAL chances we have to get an in-person sales opportunity or convert an incoming office call into a job. From that information, we can measure how many technicians we can keep busy.

2. We can measure the effectiveness of our advertising and if we are reaching the right people with the right message in the right area. It helps us become more efficient.

As shown here, we track: Net Leads, Onsite Estimate Appointments, Onsite Estimates, Conversion to Jobs, Job Tracking, Revenue Per Truck, Revenue Per Technician, and Callbacks.

Each step in the funnel is measured monthly at a minimum and weekly when we think a trend may be emerging.

The Revenue/Gas Metric

One of the best examples of a great ACTIONABLE Metric for my Home Services Business is the revenue that each technician generates in one month divided by the amount of gas they purchase in the same month. This gives me one ratio for each technician and one ratio for the entire company.

When I see the revenue/gas ratio decrease, it means the technician is spending more on gas for every dollar of revenue he's bringing in. When the metric starts to show a lower ratio for the technician compared to previous months, we first look into job location and job size to determine the cause.

But if we start seeing that ratio continue to drop the second month, our technician is probably quitting, but just hasn't told us yet. That's our experience. The revenue/gas metric has been a great predictor of whether one of my wolves is about to leave the company.

Prior to a departure, the metric indicates if our technician is losing his drive to be a contributing member of the team. If his revenue is down, then his pay is down, and it costs us more to get him to complete his jobs. We found out that those jobs with the lower metric were taking longer, creating REDOs, and eroding *The Customer Experience*, with the customer satisfaction metric being lower on those jobs as well.

The revenue/gas metric actually helps us identify and address employee behavior.

When you identify succinct and timely KPIs, you have a dashboard that allows you to improve what you measure and puts you on a path that improves the ultimate metric:

Your ROE (Return on Effort)

(HOW MUCH MONEY YOU'RE GETTING FOR THE EFFORT YOU'RE EXPENDING.)

5th … Online Reputation Management is a Necessary Activity

After being in business for eight years, I realized that Online Reviews became a huge part of my reputation management. The online review platforms were just beginning to gain momentum at the time I was launching The Trusted Toolbox, and when I looked into it, I realized that my online reputation didn't match up with my customers' experiences because, as they say: do something wrong once to one customer, and they'll tell 10 people. Do a great job for one customer, and you're lucky if they tell one person!

It takes a lot to create a raving fan, and when you achieve this, it feels AWESOME! But raving fans typically don't share their great customer experience with others.

On the other hand, fail to show up to give a free estimate, and watch that overlooked person become the town crier and rise up on their town square soap box to tell ALL the people how harmed they were with their newfound Keyboard Courage. It would never dawn on them to give you another chance, seeing how it's a free estimate! Not all people are that way though, but one could affect many.

Online reviews of your business are inevitable, unavoidable, and at times, unimaginable in their content! Regardless, I suggest you embrace the review process as early as possible. I wanted to get a handle on it and make it work for me, especially when I realized that 40 percent of our customers were coming back and doing good repeat business, but not posting reviews of their experience. So, I decided to make them part of our marketing and advertising team.

We instituted a Review Card where, at the end of a great transaction, my technicians would actually ask for a five-star review by saying to the customer …

"It would mean the world to me if you would give me a five-star review, and if I didn't earn five stars, let me know and I will make it happen!"

Making our happy customers part of our team was pure GOLD for us! A BIG nugget. Once we implemented this, our online reviews increased 300 percent. We needed to get more reviews to accurately reflect our business model and delivery.

What secures that GOLD is incenting my technicians to ask for the review using that simple statement above. Every time their job performance receives a good online review, they receive a little extra cash. That encourages my wolfpack to do a good job, ask for the review, and make sure that the customer is happy in the end.

The Positive Review Response

There's something I learned when it comes to managing your online review process and responding to reviews. When you receive a positive review, respond with thanks in the simplest of ways. You don't want to appear as if positive reviews seldom, if ever, happen. Act as if they are commonplace but always appreciated …

"Thank you for your kind words, the team really appreciates it."

"We enjoyed working with you."

"I know that (Employee Name) liked working with you as well and will enjoy hearing this.

Always share positive reviews with your team because they earned it. Moreover, it serves to reinforce the right habits with your people—from those answering the phones right through to the technician collecting payment and making *The Customer Experience* worthy of a five-star request!

The Negative Review Response

Negative reviews are a different beast all together. You can try to contact the customer, and, if allowed to interact with them, listen with the hopes of solving the wrong. But guess what---- these people don't want to engage in conflict with you. They want to use their Keyboard Courage to have their voice heard, but do NOT want to interact with anyone personally because that's uncomfortable.

You have to learn to dance with this devil of online reviews and realize that the customer will most likely not take a call or open an email from you. Chances are, you're not going to be allowed any further contact. You've heard it before and you'll hear it again, *"You can't please all of the people all of the time."*

If you can address the concerns and they're reasonable—DO IT! In a retail situation, you may need to refund money, go back and perform a service, or replace a product. These are all the costs of doing business and running a reputable company. Plan ahead and set aside a portion of your revenues for these expenses.

When I first started, I couldn't imagine giving someone a full refund. After 10 years in business, I've discovered that sometimes a full refund is the only way. If you give them their money back, all they can say is, *"That SOB gave me all my money back and didn't charge me."*

This Next Part Isn't Any Easier

You need to respond online to your customers' concerns. Take a deep breath and approach the process of responding with ZERO EMOTION. This will help get you in the right frame of mind for a professional and succinct response.

Here's an example of a response to a negative online review if The Trusted Toolbox misses an appointment:

"We apologize for this inconvenience. We are trying to earn our customers' business each day. But we missed the mark. We tried to reach you to reschedule, but if you would like to call us back, we stand ready to make this right."

The key points are to show that you put your best effort into all that you do and to show that you cared about the mistake and intend to correct it.

Here are the critical GOLD nuggets that will help you in managing negative online reviews:

- Do NOT make it personal.

- Do NOT try to argue your case in the court of public online review.

- Do NOT try to offer a resolution in this response.

- Do NOT write more than two sentences.

Here's the good news: people who read reviews look for negative ones and look for your response. They expect a solid, reputable company to have a few negative reviews. It's your response that will determine if they give you a second chance based on your overwhelmingly positive online reputation. We don't want negative reviews, but they happen. In our case, we have a good reputation online, which truly reflects the flywheel momentum of our customer experience.

6th ... My Team Didn't Know My 5/3/1

Finally, I zeroed in on the sixth element that I would need to tackle to lift me out of the rut I was in. I began redoing the painted picture of my three-year vision by asking myself:

- Where do I want the company to go over the next three years, after having been in business for eight years?

- Where do we want to be this year?

Going through the process of where we were and where we were going made me focus on what we would most likely look and perform like in the upcoming year—which happened to be our 11th year of being in business. I became detailed in explaining what our training room would look like; how we would be organized to answer phones; how scheduling of work would scale up; how the quality assurance manager role would work into the mix; the number of trucks we would need; and how many technicians we would need to man those trucks and deliver *The Customer Experience*.

Once I had the Trusted Toolbox Training Manual on paper and video, and the picture of the future of the company, I was really able to give my people something to digest and wrap their commitment around. I started to see people pick up ownership of their tasks and take up their role in the three-year vision.

I set up my first offsite meeting for the key members of my team, where we spent one Saturday morning reviewing how we performed last year and what we wanted to do this year. We broke the year down by quarters to add more specificity to what we were going to do.

Having the whole value chain of a team together and uninterrupted by ringing phones, we were able to focus on what we wanted those one-year goals to look like and to identify the key areas we needed to get focused on. Everyone knew their piece in the grand design and that would allow me to fulfill my role as the Entrepreneur so we could really start cranking.

The GOLD in all of this was getting the process out of my head and down on paper. Everyone wanted to become a part of the bigger picture I was presenting, and tackling the six areas described above and sharing it with my people allowed us to do just that.

We got out of the rut and we began to move closer to achieving operational excellence as a company with 26 employees working as one. We realized that the nucleus of our company came from everyone understanding our one-year goal, acknowledging their piece of the puzzle, and holding each other accountable in order to help our technicians shine in the field.

The final link in that chain and the lynchpin in really achieving operational excellence is the technician. It's up to them to put all of your advertising, lead conversion, and process excellence into a final positive, lasting customer experience. The key players are the technicians who have decided to give your wolfpack a shot and determine if working as part of a team makes their lives better.

YOU have to understand who they are and
WHAT MAKES THEM TICK.

Understanding the Lone Wolf

The first GOLD nugget for connecting with your wolfpack is realizing that they are exactly what you see. To borrow the catchphrase coined by the actor/comedian Flip Wilson in the late 1960s, "What You See is What You Get." WYSIWYG!

In my experience in corporate America, I often found that people have a hidden agenda for a variety of reasons that are often difficult to see. Office politics are difficult and sometimes treacherous waters to navigate because you never know what someone's agenda might be. What you see and hear may not be the real issue.

With my wolfpack, agendas are out in the open!

When they walk in and say, *"Chris, I need to make more money,"* you know they need to make more money. Period. You don't know why they need to make more money, but you know they need to. It's always real clear and straight up honest with my technicians. WYSIWYG!

When they walk in and say, *"I have a problem with this job,"* you know they have a problem with this job. There's no hidden agenda or angle they're pulling on you; you can detect exactly when they're not picking up on the training; and you can see exactly when they're not feeling fulfilled in their job. WYSIWYG!

Achieving operational excellence in our processes put us on our growth trajectory, but I needed to strengthen the final link in the chain. The last, most important part of the picture was to ensure that our technicians—who ultimately deliver the services that our customers expect—were selected, trained, managed, and incentivized correctly. For this reason, the entire next chapter is devoted to taking technicians as lone wolves and developing them into the Wolfpack.

7

Developing the Wolfpack

Hunger drives the wolf out of the wood.
—German proverb

The term Lone Wolf, as applied to a person, first appeared in the late 1890s, and is taken from an occurrence in nature. Wolves are normally pack animals, but sometimes a wolf is driven from the pack and has to survive on its own. Merriam-Webster defines "lone wolf" as "a person who prefers to work, act, or live alone."

Out in the wild, a LONE WOLF is able to fend for himself and will often do just fine on his own. When a technician thinks of joining our team, he's assessing us as a wolf would scope out a wolfpack to determine whether the environment is a good fit for him. He may be fending for himself in the wild and taking care of business, but if he senses that he can do better with less stress in this environment, he will opt into the WOLFPACK.

The first step in bringing operational excellence to this last leg of the striving for excellence journey was in identifying an assessment tool for understanding the attitudes and behaviors of the technicians and my entire team in my wolfpack. That understanding would also serve as a supportive framework for writing job descriptions for, interviewing, and training technicians. For this, I selected the DiSC Profile as a non-judgmental evaluation model to understand people's behavioral differences.[12]

The letters in the DiSC acronym stand for their four categorizations of personality types:

Dominance: People who place emphasis on results. They tend to focus on the bottom line and radiate confidence. They like seeing the big picture and getting straight to the point.

Influence: People who put importance on influencing and persuading others. They tend toward openness and dislike being ignored. They're optimistic and like collaborating with others.

Steadiness: People who tend toward cooperation. They're often sincere and dependable, but dislike being rushed. They tend to show a calm manner and are supportive of others.

Conscientiousness: People who places emphasis on quality, accuracy, and competency. They often fear being wrong and prefer to work independently.

Everyone in my wolfpack has taken the DiSC Profile and I administer it to all applicants and new hires. It provides a common language that people can use to better understand themselves and others. It helps me develop my training style and communication and training style with everyone. Most importantly, it helps me understand my technicians—how they think, interact, and react to incentives. It guides me in how to orient them and train them to give their best.

Fitting the Profile

Of course, we always strive to hire technicians who are similar to the other guys in the pack, but I don't expect my current technicians to bring in others. Remember, lone wolves don't travel in packs. It was up to me to find the technicians I wanted with well-worded job descriptions placed in ZipRecruiter, Indeed, and Craigslist.

Recall in the last chapter where I said that, with a wolfpack, WYSIWYG and their agendas are often clear and direct? Well, that's exactly how I went about writing the job description. I let them know that they would be part of a team, what the job entailed, and how much they could make. I didn't have to use big, flowery words. I just needed them to understand and apply. For some of them, it was the first job application they had ever submitted.

Here's an abbreviated example of a job description that I would use, to give you an example of the tone and language I use to attract lone wolves:

> **JOB DESCRIPTION**
>
> LEAD HANDYMAN—Contact me for a great opportunity with an outstanding home repair and remodeling company in the North Atlanta area.
>
> I don't know your name, BUT I know:
>
> - Your aspirations and that you want to continually improve yourself and your skills.
> - You want more than a job. You want a career.
> - You want more training and the opportunity to develop a wide range of skills within your craft.
>
> When you send us your resume, it will highlight your passion for what you do.
>
> When we talk, you and I will communicate about important matters, such as what you can expect from us, your career goals, and what you would like to make.

I would then phone screen applicants and schedule an interview. Be prepared to be frustrated with this process. Everything has to happen in close succession. I have to schedule interviews the same week I am phone screening, although the likelihood of a lone wolf coming out of the woods long enough for an interview is about 1 in 10. To compensate, I would schedule the interviews back-to-back so I wouldn't waste my time with the inevitable no shows.

When the applicants did arrive, I would describe my wolfpack and how we work, then ask them to assess themselves in the areas that were important to us. I would then explain the pay program in detail.

If we thought the applicant was a good fit, we would bring him in again and try him out by sending him on a job with one of our best technicians. With this process, we would usually know within three days whether he'd be a good fit with the rest of the pack, or if he'd be better off out there on his own.

Once we were able to attract, interview, and 'live test' the talent we were looking for, and we both thought it was a good fit, the next step would be onboarding the technician into the pack. We would begin our training to orient him on our mission, on the importance of *The Customer Experience*, on our operational processes, and most importantly, on our technical quality expectations.

The combination of in-house training and working with our current team in the field would help us further evaluate the new person's fit within our company. It would also help him further evaluate us. I'm always attentive to the reality that I'm onboarding a FREELANCE MINDSET and I'm training that mindset to be part of a team now.

Managing and Developing the Lone Wolf

Most of the traits of the lone wolf personality overlap with those of introverts, though they are "confident introverts" and their behavior is most often purpose-driven. They're fiercely independent, which can make onboarding a challenge. They strive to eliminate distractions and prefer to focus singularly on completing their work. They prefer quality over quantity. They're trustworthy, but can have trust issues in others.[13]

I think there's GOLD in knowing how to manage these guys correctly. Since I launched The Trusted Toolbox, I've worked with many lone wolves and I'm going to share with you my *Seven Lessons Learned* over the years in how to manage and develop these very independent individuals into a CUSTOMER FOCUSED team.

1. They Need to Think "Us", Not "Me"

One of the first things we get across to our technicians is that we expect them to be part of a team and that working WITH a pack of wolves is going to reap them far more money, less anxiety in completing the job, and greater recognition and praise than trying to carve out an existence out there on their own.

Once they come on board, we let them know that they have to develop a "we" versus "me" attitude, even if they see themselves as freelancers and brilliant technicians. We let them know that customers are buying the "team" and not just them as individuals.

We tell them that while the customer may like you, if you bad mouth your company thinking that the customer will show loyalty to you, then you are way off the mark. What the customer is really seeing is someone who doesn't deep down show loyalty to his own company, and this often prompts the customer to begin questioning the quality of the work being done. This was an especially hard lesson for one technician who came back to the office one afternoon saying,

"The customer can't stand our company but she really liked me. But don't worry, I took care of her!"

I told him, *"Well, you really did! She's not going to call us back for more work, and they have already called to complain about the experience."*

I told him that he missed out on the opportunity to finish with a flourish and flushed all the chances of getting a tip from the customer. I also said he blew his chances for a positive online review saying they can't wait to have The Trusted Toolbox and him, in particular, come back to do more work.

The guys that are a good fit will get IT. They see the value of being in a pack, getting set up for success, and creating a great customer experience. Giving our technicians that "Us" versus "Me" lens helps them recognize that they don't have to extinguish somebody else's flame to make their own shine brighter.

2. Motivate Them through Technical Training

They already think they're the smartest guys in the room, so you need to train toward that end. You need to motivate them with tips and techniques that can make them even smarter. With my wolves, if I commit to training and bore them or don't help them get better technically at their craft, they will not accept *The Customer Experience* processes that I want them to make habitual.

If you go into a training session with your pack and do nothing but weigh them down with reminders and empty clichés, such as *"call your customers … do a great job … make sure you get a signature when you're done,"* they're going to gloss over, shut down, and feel like they're wasting their time.

But if you go into a session showing them clever ways to do their job better or be more efficient in the field, they're going to be engaged and open to learning. When you interact with lone wolves, you always have to make their lives better. I tell them,

"You already think you're the smartest guy in the room, but I'm going to make you even smarter."

It doesn't have to be a huge lesson every Wednesday for my guys, just something they can put in their toolbox for later use. For instance, by using new silicone washers every time they change out P-traps in plumbing, customers won't have to call back with leak issues. Or when changing out a strike plate on a door with the screws stripped out, toothpicks or even golf tees are great little things to plug back into the screw holes—just jam them in and snap them off, and then drill in the screw.

Those two little tips have been recited back to me countless times by my technicians. It shows they are listening, but it also helps them solve a problem quicker, easier, and BETTER! That's the key: THEY GET BETTER at what they love to do.

When a great carpenter comes on board, I know that I can't spend all my time training him on what he's already proficient in, but if I can add to his skill set—one of the benefits of running with a pack—then he'll stay longer.

3. You Have to Be the Best Swordsman

People often think that pirate captains were cutthroat and commanded with an iron fist. Yet, in most historical cases, that wasn't how they ruled their ships. The real attraction of pirates to a pirate captain was the skipper's ability to get the most bounty for everybody on the ship. And they would follow that pirate captain as long as he could rake in the most riches. The crew looked up to someone who was capable of commanding and navigating a huge schooner and could get them more BOUNTY.

Of course, pirate captains had to demonstrate that they were accomplished swordsmen and accurate with a pistol. They had to be the best to put to rest any notion of someone challenging their command, for if someone did, they would have to act quickly and strike back. But a smart captain wouldn't "run the mutineer through," as the saying goes. He needed the manpower. He would instead nick the challenger on the ear with his sword to let the trouble-maker and everyone else know that THE CAPTAIN IS STILL IN CHARGE.

I don't use a sword, but I immediately let my guys know who's in charge and they respect that. They'll listen to me more. That's GOLD I can bank. They want to work for someone who's better than them and who they respect. And they'll stick with me because I can bring them more BOUNTY than they can bring on their own.

Here's a conversation I had with a technician who came to my office once to complain about how much he was making. He started by saying …

"Chris, I can't make any money here. All these estimates aren't done correctly."

I pulled out one of the estimates and said, *"Okay, let's take a look at the job you did."*

He interrupted and said, *"I'm not sure you understand."*

I said, *"Well, I completely understand because I'm the one who wrote the estimate. By the way, how come you didn't use the no-rot PVC trim?"*

I let him know that I knew about those kinds of details, and if he wanted to waste our time and complain about not doing the job correctly and blaming others, it was a wasted effort.

I remember once showing one of my new carpenters how to cut crown molding. He sat there with his mouth open and a look on his face that said, *"I thought you were just the boss."* He let everyone know that he saw the boss out getting it done and they all appreciated the effort.

You need to be confident enough to allow your shipmates to express themselves, but also let them know that you're the best swordsman on the ship and the captain who's going to help them find the GOLD.

4. You Can't Domesticate a Lone Wolf

You can get them to produce at a higher level though by letting them know they can make more money, improve their life, and reduce their stress. BUT OVER-MANAGING THEM turns them into domesticated dogs who can't solve problems on their own in the field. They begin to lose their confidence and they start to sound as if their hearts aren't in it any longer. They'll walk into my office or come up to me in the field and say,

"Chris, I need Friday off (on a Thursday), I'm really burned out."

Or you hear customers saying, *"Your guy was here today, but he didn't finish everything."*

It is a balance act managing these guys. They'll TELL you exactly what they're thinking through their actions, body language, and tone of voice (WYSIWYG) and you have to continually reinforce those behaviors that make them successful. Reinforce the FACT that by completing their job like an artist, they will get more praise, more money, and less stress in their lives. We remind them that by providing the customer with a great experience from the beginning, the customer will let them be the artist they want to be for the duration of the project.

Overloading a lone wolf with processes, constraints, and rules will lead them to become a non-problem-solving underperformer and not the artist who finishes each job with a flourish. The domesticated dog knows it doesn't have to hunt for food or look for shelter. It has a carefree life. Wolves, on the other hand, NEED to HUNT. They want to hunt. That's what satisfies them.

5. They're Experiential Learners

Most technicians in the Home Services Business are experiential learners. That means they're hands-on learners. They cannot sit in on a video conference and have me tell them to go out there and perform great customer service or watch a how-to video on their own. They would be bored and would tune out.

You wouldn't catch them reading this book either. They'll tell you that they need to experience it in order to understand it and remember it. To explain what you mean by *The Customer Experience*, you need to draw analogies that reflect THEIR experience.

Eating at Chick-fil-A, which ALL of them have experienced, has more meaning to them than staying at the Ritz Carlton, which NONE of them have experienced. This is the only way they can connect with what great customer service really means.

The analogy doesn't always have to be experienced physically though. It could represent something they can immediately identify with, such as a smiling person behind the counter or helpful person in the aisle of a home improvement store. When pointed out, they make a connection to being a responsible and accountable professional.

There's one video I use in my training sessions about a Navy pilot landing his fighter jet on an aircraft carrier and needing to "Call the Ball" when landing. It's a story my technicians love and it allows me to reinforce my point about taking responsibility for *The Customer Experience.*

When landing on a U.S. aircraft carrier, the pilot sights the lights from the multi-colored Optical Landing System, nicknamed the "meatball" or "ball." During the pilot's approach, they're told to "Call the Ball" by the Air Boss, and when they do, they let the team on the carrier know that they've <u>accepted responsibility</u> for the landing.

Pilots also know that the flight deck crew will be ready to help them get their jet secured when they land, and the team responsible for setting the tension on the arresting cable knows what they have to do.

We conclude with a video showing this well-coordinated, well-executed, complicated landing. After we finish watching the video, I look at them and let them know, in no uncertain terms, that the whole team is behind them. And I also let them know, in no uncertain terms, that when they're getting ready to go to the customer, to CALL THE BALL and take responsibility for landing *The Customer Experience.*

GUESS who's calling THEIR CUSTOMERS now!

6. Don't Play Favorites

You'll benefit from remembering this lesson I learned: when you brag on one wolf, consistently, the other wolves will develop resentment and will generally get pissed off at you. IF you think playing them against each other motivates them to do better, YOU'RE WRONG! It never works that way. While you're praising the one, the others are thinking, *"Hell, I'm better than that guy!"* or *"He's getting all the BEST jobs."*

What motivates them is seeing themselves on the board because they were the highest revenue producer, or the one who got the most positive reviews, or brought in the most additional work.

We run contests that "Gamify" the incentives and allow my guys to compete with each other because that healthy competition is great for them. Gamification of the incentives allows the lone wolves to compete and take pride in their success. The rewards are never huge monetary amounts—they are gift cards or tools, and it is amazing how hard they work for them.

We typically conduct the games over two months to allow the technicians time to see where and how they're measuring up against the others. At the end, the awards are given without fanfare or over-patronizing the winner.

7. The Rule of the Well-Placed F-Bomb

This may seem a little crude and unprofessional, and maybe it is, but one thing I have learned is that the F-bomb, if dropped at the right time, becomes more than an expletive. It becomes a bonding word. It lets my guys know I'm one of them, I'm a part of their pack, and that I speak their language. It says that I'm not a corporate weenie and not afraid to show some aggression. Generally speaking, weenies are typically not the best swordsmen.

I came out of the corporate zoo where swearing demonstrated a lack of good manners. In fact, it showed a lack of emotional awareness, and to some, a lack of intelligence. I still maintain a professional manner when interacting with customers, technicians, and my office. I don't go off like a busted hose and swear all the time.

I've found that it's important to let my guys know that I'm one of them by not only TALKING their language and WALKING their language, but by letting them know that I have their back when they follow what I've taught them.

Another video I show my technicians is of coach Rex Ryan

addressing his team before a game. They're in a large conference room and he's reviewing the game plan and giving them instructions before their pre-game meal. He's using technical language and specific nomenclature and methodically laying out the game plan for his team.

He ends his speech with, "NOW let's go eat a F*****G Snack!!!" and storms out of the room. And the team jumps up and follows him out. Now, that's a well-placed F-BOMB! Used in the right context, my language, intended to connect but also express passion, has improved the attention my technicians pay to *The Customer Experience*.

Lessons from My Grandmother

My grandmother, Helen Lalomia, was really my 'grandmentor.' Growing up, I used to spend time with my grandparents at their home in Buffalo, New York in a community called Little Italy. I loved that neighborhood. There were lots of Italian families and we were just minutes away from the Buffalo Zoo. I learned some early lessons from my grandmother during those visits that would end up helping me in the entrepreneurial wild later in my life.

The houses in Little Italy were built really close together in the 1940s in a style called "Shotgun." A Shotgun-style house is a single-story residence with a long narrow layout measuring 20 or so feet wide and two-to-four rooms deep. The living room was most always in the front of the house, followed by one or two bedrooms, with the kitchen in the back of the house.

I recall one summer when one of my friends, Johnny, was given a BB gun by his dad and we were out across the street from my grandparent's house in a school parking lot to practice shooting. Johnny pulled away for some reason I can't remember and accidentally shot my grandmother's window in the front of her shotgun-style house.

When I returned home later, my grandma, who was in a wheelchair at the time, rolled up to me and said,

"Christopher, do you know what happened to my window in the front?"

"No, grandma," I said, *"I'm not sure what you're talking about. What do you mean the window in the front? Let me go take a look."*

She then said, *"Christopher, what were you, Johnny, and Camille doing today?"*

I said, *"Well, we were just out doing nothing."*

My grandmother wasn't buying what I was selling. She rolled over to the phone, called Johnny's and Camile's moms, and had my two friends come over. She got all three of us lined up in her kitchen and then took us into the formal living room. She started asking questions, and we started squirming, and then we began singing like canaries and explained that Johnny had accidentally shot the window.

Afterwards, she told me,

> **"You want to get to the truth.**
> **You get all the liars in one room."**

She believed and instilled in me that you have to confront someone when they do something wrong. And when there's more than one party involved, you're going to get one side of the story, and then the other side of the story, and find that the two sides of the story don't add up. It promotes accountability and teamwork when you have all parties speak out together in this manner. It also saves a lot of time.

I recently had a customer issue that needed resolving and I asked the technician what the problem was. He said it began with the scheduler and started to give me all the things he was doing right and kept going on and on about himself, so I interrupted him and said, *"HOLD IT."*

Together, we walked into the scheduler's office and I turned to the technician and said, *"OK, tell me again what you just said."*

The technician didn't use all the same words, so I called him on it. Then my scheduler chimed in and said, *"Well, the estimator didn't write it up correctly and I was trying to help the technician who wasn't listening,"* and I said, *"HOLD IT."*

I called in the estimator and put the phone in the middle of the room and put it on speakerphone, and the estimator said that the initial customer request was written in the notes, which were on the work order. Problem resolved.

The technician missed the note, the scheduler missed the note, and the estimator should have been more explicit in his write up. We got right to solving the problem, as opposed to pointing blame. Pointing blame in the Home Services Business, or in any business really, doesn't solve the problem. We all realized that together, we can get further.

The other thing my grandmother used to say was,

> **"When you confront somebody and they start talking a lot, you**
> **know they're guilty."**

That was her way of saying that when you're making excuses and you're trying to talk yourself out of something, people can see it and hear it in your voice. And they don't want to hear more than one reason, because one reason may be a valid reason, but two reasons start to smell like an excuse.

My Grandmother Helen's two points are pure GOLD. You can cut right to the root of the issue, place accountability instead of blame on the right person, and produce an incredible customer experience. I will take one reason when somebody is explaining something, but if you get too many "reasons," you soon realize that excuses are flying loose.

Developing the individuals in your wolfpack takes a bit of science (DiSC Profile) and a bit of ART. Understanding your lone wolves, incentivizing them correctly, training them effectively, and measuring how well they do will get your company going in the right direction—putting your customers first, with less disruption and distraction to you and more work satisfaction for your wolves.

My journey through the wild included many areas of activities, and the training of my team was an area that I gave particular focus to after we had really started moving toward operational excellence. At that point, I became more of a trainer than a remodeler or handyman boss. In essence, I was in the training business.

8

Charting Your Path through the Wild

Success is a journey, not a destination. The doing is often more important than the outcome.

—Arthur Ashe

If you're here to read about how my story ends, guess what? It hasn't!

As I shared in Chapter 2, this is a journey *into* something, not a completion of something. This isn't the peak of the mountain I'm climbing or that you'll be climbing, for there's always another summit once you've reached the first.

I set out to write this book so you can experience the most important realizations and milestones on my journey from the gorilla in a zoo to an entrepreneur in the wild. My success story and lessons learned have hopefully given you the inspiration and encouragement to make the jump and to beat out a path, like Lewis and Clark, through the wild that lays out in front of you.

You existing business owners were also in mind when I was writing this book. My lessons learned after 12 years of working at it and succeeding in the Home Services Business can perhaps help you refine your business mindset and give you some areas to focus on to improve your company's operational excellence.

Let's review the lessons learned and GOLD nuggets found along the journey from the corporate zoo to the wild.

➜ Are You a Gorilla in a Zoo?

If this book is meant for you, then you realize that you, me, and Willie B. weren't kings at all. Our lives were defined for us. We were told what to do, when to do it, and how to do it. You've come to that realization now and you're thinking about what you'd prefer doing with your business life.

What's your definition of success? Your success depends on how you define it and on the trade-offs you're willing to not just accept, but embrace as you pursue your dream. Big GO-FAST Boats are a good status symbol, but are not always a definer of success.

What are you passionate about? What do you enjoy doing? Take some time to jot down the things that you just naturally enjoy undertaking. What makes you the happiest and makes the day sail by for you?

What are your strengths and opportunities, likes and dislikes? Your Strengths/Opportunities and Likes/Dislikes (SOLD) form a Decision Framework for evaluating your business ideas and opportunities. Your SOLD approach gives you the boundaries within which to work and creates a paradigm from which to map your decisions regarding your abilities and passions.

SOLD Decision Framework

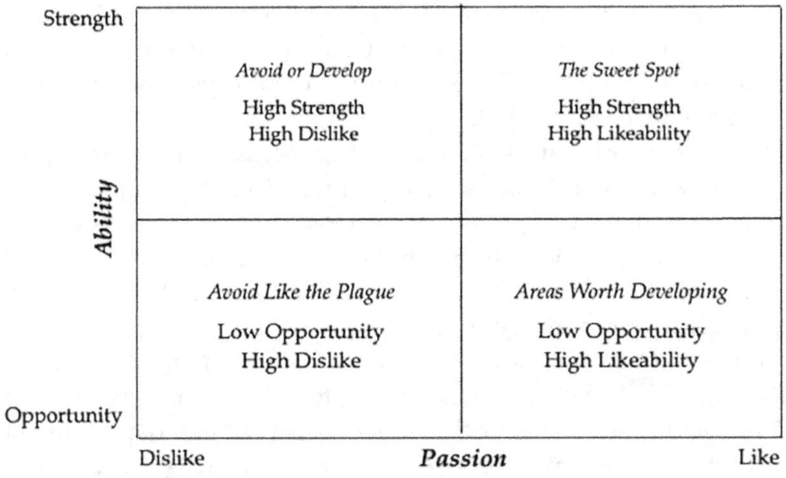
Strength
Avoid or Develop
High Strength
High Dislike
The Sweet Spot
High Strength
High Likeability
Ability
Avoid Like the Plague
Low Opportunity
High Dislike
Areas Worth Developing
Low Opportunity
High Likeability
Opportunity
Dislike
Passion
Like

Do You Have What It Takes?

There are two facets when it comes down to knowing whether or not you have what it takes: THE MENTAL and THE PHYSICAL. Two important questions to ask yourself as you consider making the jump from a corporate employee to being an entrepreneur:

MENTALLY, do you have the courage and self-confidence? Are you a risk taker? Can you solve problems? Do you have the ability to handle a bunch of things at once and the mental agility to pivot on a dime? Do you have optimism? Are you a good fighter? Are you resilient? If you get knocked down, do you keep getting back up? Bottom line: do you have a good idea and are you ready to BET on YOU?

PHYSICALLY, do you have the resources? You've become accustomed to whatever your lifestyle is today. Making this leap will most likely be uncomfortable for you and your family. You and they may be facing a potentially drastically different lifestyle for the next few years. Have you saved up enough? Most importantly, have you checked in with the family?

SIDE HUSTLES don't work in the Home Services Business. If you're halfway in, you're all the way out. With "one foot on the platform and one foot on the train," you'll have the first leg of your journey filled with frustration and misfortune. Your side hustle will most likely never make the money you think it's going to make. It will never show you fully the opportunity and potential of your idea.

➜ Have an Escape Plan

Write a full business plan for how you'll succeed on the outside. Moreover, the best time to put one together is before you leave the corporate zoo. It'll help you create a mindset focused on what exactly it is that you're running toward.

If you're thinking of jumping with only a few ideas on a couple of pages, then you're destined to be ONE of the NINE-OUT-OF-TEN who fail for not having flushed out all of the thoughts and details swirling around in your head. You're not doing justice to yourself or your family by not defining your product, your market, and your operations.

Shop the idea. The process of writing a business plan gives you the added advantage of being able to shop your idea and make it an even better one. This is a HUGE benefit that shouldn't be overlooked. When you shop your idea, you're getting advice and feedback from people who've been there and have more knowledge and experience than you do.

It's not the exercise of writing the plan that's important. IT'S THE GOLD that you're mining from the feedback and ideas they'll share with you that you can fold back into your business plan.

Find a mentor or several mentors. Successful entrepreneurs love to tell you about themselves and their realizations and victories if asked the right way. Ask the kinds of questions that allows them to share how they shot the bear, or how they saved a customer, or how they broke into a new niche on a shoestring budget. They'll tell stories filled with GOLD nuggets of valuable information.

Prepare and ask purposeful, pointed questions so you can get detailed answers in return. Use their time wisely and don't abuse the help that you're seeking. The detailed questions will allow you to uncover the potential Strengths, Weaknesses, Opportunities, and Threats in your plan. A mentor's help in defining these for you and helping you through your issues and opportunities will help make you a stronger leader and a better business operator.

→ Know the Importance of *The Customer Experience*

I learned that *The Customer Experience* is MORE important than the quality of the work itself. Customers want to feel good about the entire process and will even overlook the quality of your product or service … if they FEEL GOOD.

The GOLD here is truly recognizing that your customers are NOT Cheap, Lazy, or Stupid. Change your mindset. Help educate them to make a smart buying decision that will be the least stressful path for them in the long run. Your customers want to go with somebody who makes them feel good about what they're doing. And you have to give them a good feeling that you know what you're doing. *The Customer Experience* starts from the first call and continues all the way through to the final walkthrough.

Strive to understand the general public's mindset and share the secrets you discover with your technicians. Let them know what's going on in the customer's mind the minute they ring the doorbell. Knowing what the customer is thinking and why places your technicians on the same playing field as their customers so they can feel confidence in themselves and competence in their work. These are the three secrets that I discovered and share with my technicians:

The 3 Secrets of the Customer

1. *Service should be completed at the time of the transaction.* My technicians are trained to KNOW that the customer's expectation is that the JOB is OVER as soon as they show up! Therefore, they don't waste the customer's time. In less than five minutes, they walk through the job with the customer, confirm the work to be done, explain their plan to do the work, and get to work—all with a smile.

2. *People buy from people they like.* I tell my guys to show up with CONFIDENCE and make eye contact with a pleasant face. This lets the customer know that you know what you're doing. Tell them your plan and how you're going to take care of them. By doing this little introduction, the customer will allow the technician to do his work and be the artist he wants to be.

3. *People will discount a purchase by ½ the price and double the amount of rebate offered.* After working with the general public in retail for many years, I've come to the conclusion that they are generally CHRONICALLY UNIFORMED. You're dealing with different personalities, different interpretations of words, and different expectations. Differences are the spice of life, but not managing them appropriately can cost you money. Getting agreement on pricing and scope upfront sets your people up for success at the end and creates a five-star customer experience.

→ Aim for Operational Excellence

You're starting to run your business with the intent of aiming for operational excellence in everything you do. What will distinguish you is your awareness of the importance of *The Customer Experience* and building your operations around delivering great customer transactions every day. Now you need to embark on figuring out what excellence in delivery really looks like and what it takes to be the ONE-OUT-OF-TEN who succeeds.

Build Momentum. Jim Collin's Flywheel Effect illustrates that good-to-great transformations never happen overnight. They're the result of a relentless pushing of a great flywheel, turn upon turn, building momentum.

As you begin, you'll start to figure out who your best customers are and you'll learn what operational excellence looks like when you have a great transaction and everything goes right for the customer. Momentum will start to work for you as each turn of the flywheel builds upon work done earlier, accumulating your investment of effort. Aim to make every turn of the wheel a great customer experience that is excellently executed.

The GOLD HERE is found in each turn of Flywheel—Confidence building Competence building Confidence building Competence. Take an account each time of what it took to score so high; make that mindset and process a habit; and replicate it on every turn of the flywheel.

Build Good Habits. As you start to scale, you'll seek out people who have the same values and habits you do. Build their competence and confidence in those habits. The more confident my technicians are, the better they are at their craft. They'll see the momentum starting to happen for them, allowing them to accumulate *their* investment of effort and realize their personal and professional objectives.

Come to Terms with Yourself. As your momentum builds, you as the business owner will have to reconcile what your role will be as your infant business grows to adolescence and entrepreneurial maturity. This is you coming to terms with yourself—realizing the things that you'll need to let go of so your child can function and thrive on its own and you can be the Entrepreneur who continues to build on the company's momentum. You can only let go of the managerial and technical tasks if you have the right processes in place and know that they're being practiced habitually by your people.

Don't Be Lulled into Complacency. Once you've nailed down your processes and your people reflect your values and habits without you having to be there, your flywheel will begin to pick up speed. That feeling of success can lull you into a state of satisfaction and possible stagnation.

You may be aiming for operational excellence every day, but never really achieving it. Therefore, you can't take your eye off the ball. You have to be on the hunt for continuous improvement with a specific focus now on driving down expenses and increasing net profits.

➔ Achieve Operational Excellence

Develop the discipline to go back each year to review your business plan, update the numbers, and sharpen the strategies. Analyze where you're performing well and where you need to make improvements. Began to work on the next level processes that will take your company to GREATNESS.

Translate your mission statement into something everyone can experience and remember. Your mission statement is really the attitude and direction you want your team to adopt every day.

Create a Mission Plaque that everyone can see. When I reinforced its message through bonus incentive programs, the words started to gel with my people. Once I translated the mission statement to the mission plaque and put incentives behind it, we started to pick up traction in being able to train around those values. All the employees began to connect with what was expected.

Document your processes and procedures. It's up to you to give your people the framework and the tasks to follow. That way you can ensure that you will get the desired outcome.

Know your key performance indicators. Put together a dashboard that allows you to have your "hands on the wheel" to know if you're heading in the right direction, your speed, and how efficiently you're performing. It also alerts to you the areas that need to be addressed and trends to be aware of, so you can begin to get your tools on these areas and get them fixed.

Make sure your team knows your 5/3/1. Once the future of your company is planned out, give your people something to digest and wrap their commitment around. They will pick up ownership of their tasks and take up their role in the three-year vision. Everyone wants to become part of the bigger picture.

The final link in the chain and the lynchpin really in achieving operational excellence in the Home Services Business is the technician, and the first and biggest GOLD nugget in understanding and connecting with your wolfpack is realizing that with blue-collar technicians, What You See is What You Get (WYSIWYG).

➔ Develop and Manage Your Wolfpack

My pack are lone wolves and they fit that profile in many ways—both good and bad. Lone wolves have positive attributes. They are confident introverts and their behavior is most often purpose-driven.

They're fiercely independent, which can make onboarding a challenge. They strive to eliminate distractions and prefer to focus singularly on completing their work. They prefer quality over quantity. They're trustworthy, but can have trust issues with others.

I think there's GOLD in how to manage these guys correctly. Since I launched The Trusted Toolbox, I've worked with many lone wolves and am sharing with you my **Seven Lessons Learned** in how to manage, develop, and coalesce freelance mindsets.

1.   They Need to Think "Us," Not "Me"

2.   Motivate Them through Technical Training

3.   You Have to Be the Best Swordsman

4.   You Can't Domestic a Lone Wolf

5.   They're Experiential Learners

6.   Don't Play Favorites

7.   The Rule of the Well-Placed F-Bomb

Foundational Success Skills

In Chapter 1, I shared how the great ape, Willie B., brought me to realize that I too was a gorilla in a zoo, not being all that I could be. I then asked ...

"Do you have what it takes to make the Entrepreneurial Leap into the wild?"

Do you have what it takes PHYSICALLY to leave corporate America and start a small business and withstand the shock to your financials and way of life? Do you have what it takes MENTALLY? Do you have a good idea to run toward and the courage and self-confidence to see it through? Are you a risk taker and a fighter? Do you have the resilience to get back up if you're knocked down and the mental agility to keep your head on a swivel and pivot on a dime?

Looking back to 12 years ago when I first made that Leap, I discovered I had what it takes. Sure, the physical was challenging and difficult to calculate, but I always had the mental. I had and still have that self-belief and stamina, and became one of the ONE-OUT-OF-TEN small businesses that hasn't failed but succeeded.

Over the course of those years, I expanded the MENTAL component of what it takes to include what I today consider to be the *Foundational Success Skills for Thriving in the Wild*:

Vision. This is the thing inside of you that guides you and gives you a sense of purpose and a desire to grow and improve. Vision brings you views of what is possible. Your vision can motivate employees to act with the same passion and purpose you have. It can ensure that everyone is working toward the same goal. Most importantly, YOU have to believe in your vision to be able to hold onto it in good and bad times.

A Plan. You may have heard the quote, *"Failing to plan is planning to fail."* It basically means that if you don't put a business plan in place and follow that plan, you can bank on being ONE of the NINE-OUT-OF-TEN small businesses that fail. You have to be plan driven and treat your business plan as a living document.

Drive. You MUST BE a highly-motivated person to make it in the wild. You're going to need energy and an indefatigable ambition to achieve. You need to be the tenacious one. You can't wait for someone else to take the initiative. Your drive can be contagious, especially among a wolfpack. You have to motivate your employees to maintain that Flywheel Momentum and make them see and believe in your vision. Look, you can have all the business smarts in the world, but without the drive to succeed, you're doomed to fail.

Self-Awareness. This skill is being able to focus on yourself and how your thoughts and actions do or do not align with your values and personal standards. If you're self-aware, you can objectively evaluate yourself and recognize how others see you. You can manage your emotions in both good and bad times. You can check yourself before you go off like a busted hose. The key is to make sure that your behavior reflects your values and intentions. This will allow you to manage your people and your business at a much higher level.

Problem Solver. You have to love solving problems, because you're going to have them! You have to be comfortable getting in the weeds and figuring out solutions. Even on a smaller scale, problem solving is a critical component for leaders who want to eliminate barriers that can hinder their people's success or their company's progress. In a *Harvard Business Review* study about the skills that influence a leader's success, problem solving ranked third out of 16 after "inspires and motivates others" and "displays high integrity and honesty."[14]

Accountability. Being an accountable leader and insisting on accountability from your team drives results. It means that you have the resolve to own up to the commitments and promises that you have made. When my employees are encouraged to take ownership of *The Customer Experience,* they know the part they play is important and they engage in their work with more purpose and passion. Build a culture of accountability and you'll promote self-reliance and confidence in your people.

Resilience. Surviving the wild requires a lot from startups today. You have to embrace the suck. By that I mean that you have to be able to trudge through something that you don't like doing in order to get to the other end so that you can move on to the next thing. Resilience, also called mental toughness or grit, is "bouncing back" after something knocks you down and sticking with it in the face of a challenge.

Resilience is solving the problem in the face of adversity.

Positive Attitude. Leadership is being able to inspire people at all times, and the key to this is your attitude. A positive outlook around your team improves their performance and motivation. It strengthens their resilience and optimism and improves problem solving. Yet, it's more than that.

A positive attitude is a requirement for addressing one of The Three Secrets of the Customer in Chapter 4, *People Buy from People They Like!* My phone ladies know the value of being personable and smiling through the phone. And my technicians know to smile and be personable when they get to the job site to do the work.

Your Attitude Determines Your Altitude

I remember when I was very young my mom would read to me *"Alexander and the Terrible, Horrible, No Good, Very Bad Day."* It was, and still is, a very popular children's picture book about a young boy named Alexander who is having a really bad day, beginning with waking up to gum in his hair from having gone to bed the night before with that piece of gum in his mouth. The story continues throughout the day with things going terrible and horrible, and ends with his mom reminding him that all people have 'bad days' no matter where they live or who they are.[15]

The moral of the story that my mom made sure I understood as I grew was that Alexander wasn't just a victim of his bad luck … that sometimes he was the one creating his own bad luck. Just as a reminder when I was having a bad day and on a downward spiral, my mom would change the title to *"Christopher and the Terrible, Horrible, No Good, Very Bad Day."*

I think that's how it all started for me. My mom helped set a foundation in me of a positive attitude and the belief that my attitude determines my altitude—how much I can achieve. If your attitude is negative, you won't be able to reach the heights that you're capable of achieving. You'll never give yourself a chance. You'll forever see yourself as a victim of everything that goes awry.

On the other hand, if your outlook is positive, anything that goes wrong and sideways is just the next challenge and an opportunity to make something right, make it better, and grow.

Your ALTITUDE in life will be determined by your ATTITUDE on life.

The Word of the Year

I was introduced to the concept of the Word of the Year several years ago and adopted it for myself ever since. It's been a valuable tool for me that I want to leave with you now as a closing thought. The word of the year serves as my guidepost. It keeps me from drifting, helps pick me up after a "Terrible, Horrible, No Good, Very Bad Day," and puts me back on my path.

The Word of the Year is easy to remember, yet for most, is hard to live up to and maintain as a guidepost. For instance, if your word of the year is "Health" and you want to get in shape, you set goals for yourself, revive good habits you once had, or begin new ones. Nobody ever 'drifts' into getting into shape. They work hard at it and, most important, they maintain the right attitude.

I had the right attitude, so the word of the year for me in 2020 was ALTITUDE. I was going to raise my company to new heights and start another business and make a difference in another group of people's lives. Then COVID-19 HIT, like a storm across the entire world, pummeling everyone.

It took some time to adjust, pivot, and re-focus and continue to strive for a higher Altitude, but we were able to react and adjust to the pandemic and are now having a great year in home services as a result. I started a new business and am committed to its success. I even wrote this book.

Reflecting on my 12-year journey, across all the good and bad experiences and struggles I shared with you in this book, and many more, what never crossed my mind was going back to the comfort and safety of the Corporate Zoo. My views on success are still evolving, as I discover new things about myself that would never have been revealed if I didn't plan my escape and stay the course. You'll discover new capabilities and strengths in yourself as well once you make the Leap!

Out here in the Wild, I'm free to live and thrive under my own steam and am betting on myself. I'm able to look at my family and say that we've made it. With all of the challenges and unknowns, I'm happier now more than ever before, but still not content. I still have goals that I want to achieve and new things that I want to learn. My journey is not ending, only continuing. And though I like my current altitude, I'm still setting my sights on the next adventures that I'll create.

If you're still with me here at the end of the book, then you're definitely a Gorilla and I hope my story inspires you to make the Leap from the Zoo to the Wild. Your journey then is just beginning. Know what you're running toward, have a plan for surviving and succeeding, and make sure you have what it takes mentally and physically. Do this, and you'll be creating your own adventures and find yourself, as I did, to be the ONE-OUT-OF-TEN who succeeded!

My last GOLD nugget of encouragement to you ... change your ATTITUDE AND ELEVATE YOUR ALTITUDE!

References

1   Pilon, Annie (July 22, 2020). *67% of Companies Expect Work from Home to Be Permanent or Long-Lasting.* Small Business Trends. Retrieved from, https://smallbiztrends.com/2020/06/work-from-home-permanently-survey.html

2   Porch Research (July 21, 2020). *Survey: Home Improvement Trends in the Time of Covid.* Porch Research. Retrieved from, https://porch.com/advice/home-improvement-trends-covid

3   ibid

4   Khurana, Simran (August 8, 2019). *Unforgettable Morpheus Wisdom from The Matrix,* ThoughtCo. Retrieved from, https://www.thoughtco.com/morpheus-wisdom-quotes-from-the-matrix-2832834

5   Griffith, Erin (September 25, 2014). *Why Startups Fail, According to Their Founders.* Fortune. Retrieved from, https://fortune.com/2014/09/25/why-startups-fail-according-to-their-founders/

6   Claritas 360 Consumer Segmentation. Claritas Research. Retrieved from, https://claritas360.claritas.com/mybestsegments/

7   Atlanta Lawn Tennis Association. *About ALTA.* Retrieved from, https://www.altatennis.org/aboutALTA.aspx

8   https://www.jimcollins.com/concepts/the-flywheel.html

9   Gerber, Michael E. (October 14, 2004). *The E-Myth Revisited: Why Most Small Businesses Don't Work and What to Do About It.* New York: Harper Business, p9. Retrieved from, https://www.amazon.com/Myth-Revisited-Small-Businesses-About/dp/0887307280/ref=sr_1_1?dchild=1&keywords=emyth&qid=1601139088&sr=8-1

10 Wickman, Gino (September 5, 2017). *What the Heck Is EOS?: A Complete Guide for Employees in In Companies Running on EOS.* BenBella Books: Dallas. Retrieved from, https://www.amazon.com/What-Heck-EOS-Employees-Companies/dp/194464881X/ref=sr_1_2?dchild=1&keywords=eos&qid=1602013338&s=books&sr=1-2

11 Wickman, Gino (April 3, 2012). *Traction: Get a Grip on Your Business*. BenBella Books: Dallas. Retrieved from, https://www.amazon.com/Traction-Get-Grip-Your-Business/dp/1936661837/ref=pd_bxgy_img_2/139-2893097-5491021?_encoding=UTF8&pd_rd_i=1936661837&pd_rd_r=267faa3d-5aae-4c0d-a981-87ad051a2755&pd_rd_w=wOAB0&pd_rd_wg=Um3ix&pf_rd_p=ce6c479b-ef53-49a6-845b-bbbf35c28dd3&pf_rd_r=44HJWQ8XQQNN9N8D25SX&psc=1&refRID=44HJWQ8XQQNN9N8D25SX

12 DiSC Profile. *DiSC Overview*. Retrieved from, https://www.discprofile.com/what-is-disc/overview/

13 Life Falcon. *Lone Wolf Personality Characteristics*. Retrieved from, https://lifefalcon.com/lone-wolf-personality-characteristics/

14 Zenger, Jack, Folkman, Joseph (July 30, 2014). *The Skills Leaders Need at Every Level*. Harvard Business Review. Retrieved from, https://hbr.org/2014/07/the-skills-leaders-need-at-every-level

15 Viorst, Judith (July 15, 1987). *Alexander and the Terrible, Horrible, No Good, Very Bad Day*. New York: Atheneum Books. Retrieved from, https://www.amazon.com/Alexander-Terrible-Horrible-Good-Very/dp/0689711735/ref=sr_1_2?crid=PWUJ847941EE&dchild=1&keywords=alexander+and+the+horrible+no+good+very+bad+day&qid=1603804712&sprefix=Alexander%2Caps%2C172&sr=8-2